AT MY TABLE

ALSO BY NIGELLA LAWSON

HOW TO EAT
The pleasures and principles of good food

HOW TO BE A DOMESTIC GODDESS
Baking and the art of comfort cooking

NIGELLA BITES

NIGELLA FRESH

FEAST
Food that celebrates life

NIGELLA EXPRESS
Good food fast

NIGELLA CHRISTMAS
Food, family, friends, festivities

NIGELLA KITCHEN
Recipes from the heart of the home

NIGELLISSIMA
Easy Italian-inspired recipes

SIMPLY NIGELLA
Feel good food

AT MY TABLE

A celebration of home cooking

NIGELLA LAWSON

FLATIRON
BOOKS

NEW YORK

AT MY TABLE. Copyright © 2017 by Nigella Lawson. Photography copyright © 2017 by Jonathan Lovekin. All rights reserved. Printed in the United States of America. For information, address Flatiron Books, 175 Fifth Avenue, New York, N.Y. 10010.

www.flatironbooks.com

Design and Art Direction: Caz Hildebrand
Cooking Assistant: Hettie Potter
Editorial Assistant: Zoe Wales
Props: Sanjana Lovekin
Cover Photography: David Ellis
Cover and endpaper pattern design: Apacuka Ceramics

The Library of Congress Cataloging-in-Publication Data is available upon request.

ISBN 978-1-250-15428-6 (hardcover)
ISBN 978-1-250-15427-9 (ebook)

Our books may be purchased in bulk for promotional, educational, or business use. Please contact your local bookseller or the Macmillan Corporate and Premium Sales Department at 1-800-221-7945, extension 5442, or by email at MacmillanSpecialMarkets@macmillan.com.

Originally published in the UK by Chatto & Windus, an imprint of Vintage

First U.S. Edition: April 2018

10 9 8 7 6 5 4 3 2

in memory of
Ed Victor

CONTENTS

INTRODUCTION

When I moved into my first home, before I did anything else, I bought a table, a table not just to eat at, but to live around.

I read recently that when NASA originally designed their spaceships, they didn't put in a table: it wasn't thought necessary, and it was hard to see how it would work; without gravity, the food would just float off it. But, as Mary Roach wrote in *Packing for Mars*, the astronauts did mind, and asked for one to be put in, even if it meant strapping on a tray, with food Velcroed to it. In the alienating isolation of space, they wanted, they said, "to sit around a table at the end of the day and eat like humans."

A table is more than a piece of furniture, just as food is more than fuel. "It seems to me," wrote M.F.K. Fisher, "that our three basic needs, for food and security and love, are so mixed and mingled and entwined that we cannot straightly think of one without the others." Around a table is where these three things meet. Our lives are formed by memories, and the focus of mine is the food I've cooked and the people I've cooked for, the people who have sat at my table, as well as the other tables I've eaten at, from the blue formica table of my childhood, to the mottled zinc one that is the nexus of my life now.

This book, like all the books I've written and all the cookbooks I've read, is not just a manual, but a collection of stories and a container of memories. But then, any recipe ever written, any meal ever eaten, is a story, the story of home cooking which, in turn, is about who we are, where we've come from and the lives that we've lived, and what we say to each other—all those assertions of love, friendship, hospitality, hope—when we invite people to sit at our table and eat the food we've made for them.

Personal history, the weaving of memories that sum up a life, social history, the story of how a culture most intimately expresses itself, a cookbook can be about all these things and more, but at its core, it answers that important, everyday question: "What are we going to eat?"

The food in this book—which comes from my kitchen, is eaten at my table, and will be eaten at yours—is the food I have always loved cooking. It doesn't require technique, dexterity, or expertise, none of which I lay claim to. Life is complicated; cooking doesn't have to be. It doesn't matter how many cookbooks I write or how many times I am erroneously called a chef, I will never be a professional. But then, no one needs qualifications to cook, or human beings would have fallen out of the evolutionary loop a long time ago. I cook, as you do, to feed myself, my family, my friends. A home cook is not a lesser being than a chef, though a markedly different one. I hate hearing people describe themselves as "just" a home cook. We may not have the technical proficiency of a chef, but why should this matter? We cook to bring pleasure, comfort, and flavor to life, to the table. This is not to say we operate in bumbling chaos, although I have learned over the years that I need a certain amount of this. In a sense, a recipe is a way of finding order in the mess of life. It's a guide, something to hold on to. And because of this, it must always be reliable, and as exact as possible, even if cooking itself can never be a precise art. There is a lot of snobbery about giving exact measurements – as if they impede the creativity of the real cook – but I do need the recipes I write (and the recipes I read) to provide as reliable and straightforward a guide as possible, without denying the spontaneity of cooking. So, please do not become hamstrung by weights and measures; I freely admit that cooking itself demands a certain cavalier attitude towards both. If you want to use 6 carrots in a stew, when I have stipulated 4, that's fine, but there needs to be a framework in the first instance, and often there can be a significant discrepancy in the weights of particular ingredients, so an entirely laissez-faire attitude would not be helpful. In baking, of course, absolute precision is a prerequisite; in cooking there can be more freedom of movement.

But no matter how specific the amount given – both in general and, in particular, of spices, herbs, salt, citrus, and so on – nothing can do the job of your palate. You cannot cook without tasting, and you need to taste, taste, taste, and taste again. A recipe can be an idea, a starting point, but when I write one, I need to know I'm giving you the tools to share the food I make. And for me, too, a recipe is the way I share my enthusiasms. I repeat certain ingredients unashamedly. The home cook has to, and happily. If I buy a jar of preserved lemons, say, for a particular recipe, or require you to, it wouldn't occur to me to leave that opened jar in the fridge with nothing else to do with it. And, indeed, it is finding ways to use up such a jar that is in itself inspiring. A home cook may work with a much more limited pantry than a chef, but still, we do discover new ingredients, and they inject new flavors into the food we cook. Home cooking isn't about treating food as a museum piece or an empty exercise in nostalgia. So many of the recipes here are drawn from meals I remember, the food I've eaten at various stages in my life, but in evoking memories, I'm also making them part of how I live and eat now.

Perhaps it is slightly churlish of me, but I admit that there is an always forthcoming question I have come to dread when I tell people I'm working on a new book or have just written one. It is "What's the theme?" Part of me wants to answer "Cooking doesn't need to have a theme, any more than life has a theme," or "The theme is the food I love cooking and like eating," though I feel the book's subtitle – a celebration of home cooking – says this more graciously. And the book's structure, or lack of it, reflects this too. All cooking, all life, is part of a continuum and, as this book came into being, I felt I didn't want to interfere with the honest jumble. The messiness of having no chapters, no breaks in the run of recipes felt so much more like the way I actually cook and live. Of course, there has to be some order; there is a flow to the recipes which, once the book was finished, I tried to impose without losing a certain random quality. "Life can only be understood backwards; but it must be lived forwards," and this Kierkegaardian premise holds true here, too. That's to say, I tried to keep the "living forwards" element intact. To those who like clear delineations and neat order, I apologize; but I breathe easier without either. And I felt emboldened by the different approach of the ebook. I'd been checking a recipe in a book of mine in ebook form, and found the list of recipes at the beginning enormously helpful. There's no reason why this should just be a feature of a digital format, and so I have happily imported that idea here.

Any food writer I've ever spoken to has always agreed that while coming up with recipe ideas is easy – we all tend to have a natural greed that invites us to think obsessively about what we want to eat and cook – giving a clear indication of how many each recipe is intended to feed is confoundingly difficult. I've written about my hesitancy in this area before: when having people over to eat, I am always stricken with fear that there won't be enough food; there are always leftovers. But that's the way I like it, and that's how a home should be. Knowing there's always something in the fridge to eat without having to cook afresh not only makes life easier, it gives a sense of security and comfort.

My portions are generous, that I freely admit; I am never knowingly undercatered. But the problem I have settling on a serving size to give for each recipe is more than just a personal neurosis. There simply cannot be any precise or absolute formula to rely on when deciding. How old are the eaters? How large are their appetites? What else are they eating at the same meal? How big was the meal they ate earlier in the day? How large the plates are that they're eating off will make a difference to the portion sizes, too.

Of course, some recipes make deciding on serving sizes relatively easy, though this is generally if they are to feed one or two people. Elsewhere, I have tried to give a range of, say, 4–6 or 6–8, to show that there is room for maneuver and to guide you – which is always what I prefer to do – rather than bark instructions.

But, as I said above: I always err on the side of generosity, believing that, whether in the kitchen or out of it, this is a happier way to be.

TURKISH EGGS

If I hadn't eaten the Turkish eggs at Peter Gordon's restaurant, The Providores, I most certainly wouldn't be tempted by the idea of poached eggs on Greek yogurt. I say that only to preempt any hesitancy on your part. For *çilbir*, pronounced "chulburr," is a revelation and a complete sensation.

If you can't get the Aleppo pepper, also known as *pul biber* or Turkish red pepper flakes, which has a mild, almost sweet heat and a distinctive lemoniness, you could substitute paprika, adding a pinch of crushed red pepper flakes. But, in these days of online grocery shopping, I'd encourage you to go for the real thing.

If you have an egg-poaching method of your own that you're perfectly happy with, ignore my instructions below. But if you're interested, this is how I, having tried just about every way in order to overcome an almost pathological fear of egg poaching, go about it. I know the business of putting the eggs in a strainer seems like a fussy step too far (and I admit I don't always follow my own instructions), but here's the thing: the crucial element in creating beautifully formed poached eggs is how fresh they are, as the longer they sit after they've been laid, the more watery the egg whites become. And since a freshly laid egg is generally held to be one that has been laid no longer than 48 hours before it's cooked, I very much doubt the eggs I buy at the supermarket count. If you gently crack an egg into a fine-mesh strainer and swirl it over a bowl, the wateriness (which turns into a stringy kind of fluff while cooking) drips away, and the gelled white that remains holds its shape more. Having said that, I do think that unless you've worked the brunch station at a busy restaurant for months on end, you'll be hard pushed to turn out perfectly formed poached eggs every time. So do not feel that anything less than perfection is a mistake, and accept a little straggliness here and there.

It is not advisable to make ahead/store

1   Fill a wide-ish saucepan (I use one of 9 inches diameter) with water to come about 1½ inches up the sides of the pan. Put it on the heat and cover so that it heats up faster. Line a large plate with some paper towels, get out a slotted spoon, and put both near the pan now.

2   Now fill another saucepan – on which a heatproof bowl can sit comfortably – again with water to come 1½ inches up the sides, and bring to a boil. Put the yogurt in said bowl, stir in the garlic and

SERVES 2

Plain whole milk Greek yogurt – ¾ cup

Garlic – 1 clove, peeled and minced

Sea salt flakes or kosher salt – 1 teaspoon

Unsalted butter – 2 tablespoons

Extra-virgin olive oil – 1 tablespoon

Aleppo pepper/Turkish red pepper flakes – 1 teaspoon

Eggs – 2 large, fridge-cold

Lemon – 2 teaspoons of juice

Dill – a few fronds, chopped

To serve:

Sourdough or other bread – chunkily sliced and toasted

salt, and sit it on top of this pan, making sure the base of the bowl doesn't touch the water. Stir it until it gets to body temperature and has the consistency of lightly whipped cream. Turn off the heat and leave the bowl as it is, over the pan.

3   Melt the butter gently in a small saucepan until it is just beginning to turn a hazelnutty brown (this is why, in classic French cuisine, it's known as *beurre noisette*), but make sure it's not actually burning. Turn the heat off under the pan, then stir in the olive oil, followed by the beautiful red pepper flakes; it will foam up fierily. Leave to one side while you get on with the eggs. And this is when you should be thinking of putting the toast on.

4   When you are ready to poach the eggs, crack the first egg into a fine mesh strainer suspended over a small bowl, then lift it up a little and swirl gently for about 30 seconds, letting the watery part of the white drip into the bowl. Gently tip the egg into a small cup or ramekin and, aiming for the white, add 1 teaspoon of lemon juice; I know everyone else says vinegar, but I just don't like the taste of it on the egg, and the lemon does the trick just the same. Proceed as above with the second egg.

5   When the poaching water is just starting to simmer, take a cup or ramekin in each hand and gently slide in the eggs, one on each side of the pan. Turn the heat right down so there is no movement in the water whatsoever, and poach the eggs for 3–4 minutes until the whites are set and the yolks still runny. Transfer the eggs with your slotted spoon to the paper-lined plate to remove any excess water. Do remember to switch off the heat. Sorry to state the obvious, but I have too often left it on this low without noticing.

6   Divide the warm creamy yogurt between two shallow bowls, top each with a poached egg, pour the peppery butter around and slightly over the yogurt, scatter the chopped dill on top, and eat dreamily, dipping in some thick well-toasted bread as you do so.

WAFFLES

I was watching an American TV show recently and missed a lot of the plot, as I was distracted by the amount of waffle-eating going on. I tried to prevent myself getting a waffle iron; I'd made that mistake once before. Reader, I didn't succeed. But I vowed that this time I wouldn't use it once then consign it to a cupboard under the stairs, and I've been as good as my word and have turned into something of a weekend waffler.

How long you cook the waffles for, as well as how many you make, will depend on the waffle iron you're using. Mine is a sturdy, non-stick stove-top Belgian waffle iron, which takes one cup of batter per batch; if you're operating a different machine, follow the directions for quantities and cooking times that come with it.

I advise you to preheat your oven to 200°F before you start so that you can put the waffles on a wire rack over a baking sheet as you make them, to keep them warm. This also helps to give them a lovely crisp crust.

For make ahead/store notes see p.274

For make ahead/store notes see p.274

I GET 5 BATCHES OUT OF MY IRON, WHICH SEPARATE INTO 20 SMALL SQUARE WAFFLES

Whole milk – 1¾ cups plus 2 tablespoons
All-purpose flour – 1¾ cups
Baking powder – 2 teaspoons
Sugar – 3 tablespoons
Fine sea salt – ¼ teaspoon
Eggs – 3 large, separated
Vegetable oil – ½ cup
Vanilla extract – 1 teaspoon

To serve:
Maple syrup
Blueberries, or other berries, as wished

1   Pour the milk into a large pitcher.

2   Combine the flour, baking powder, sugar, and salt in a bowl. Put the egg whites into another – grease-free – bowl ready to whisk, and add the yolks to the milk pitcher.

3   Add the oil and vanilla to the pitcher of milk and yolks and beat together, then whisk the egg whites, ready and waiting in their bowl, until you have firm peaks.

4   Pour the pitcher of wet ingredients into the bowl of dry ones, and whisk together, making sure there are no lumps (a little hand whisk is fine for this), then fold in the beaten egg whites slowly, gently, and thoroughly until you have a thick, smooth, and airy batter.

5   Heat the waffle iron following the instructions (some need to be lightly oiled before you start). The one I use requires you to separate the halves and put each on a separate ring to heat up first.

6   Fill one side of your heated waffle iron with 1 cup (or appropriate amount) of batter and close with the other heated half of the waffle

iron. Cook for 1 minute, then turn the waffle iron over and cook on the other side for 2 minutes. If you're using an electric waffle iron, you will obviously not be turning it over, so you may need to cook for a minute or so longer. Just follow the instructions that come with the iron in all cases.

7   Ease the cooked waffle out of the waffle iron. Keep going until all the batter is used up. If you're not keeping the waffles warm in the low oven (see recipe introduction) each waffle should be eaten just as soon as it comes out of the iron. Generously pour maple syrup over your waffle, and tumble a few berries alongside if wished.

EGG TORTILLA PIE

This recipe for an easy, throw-it-all-together supper or bolstering weekend breakfast comes from my longtime kitchen companion, Hettie Potter, and very grateful I am, too. Impressively, she makes this a single portion. I, no modest eater, feel it is perfectly substantial for two, though it is a little tricky to divide.

Think of this as a pie that uses flour tortillas in place of pie crust and, although I have given precise measures for what to chuck in, consider them guidance only. The same goes for the ingredients themselves: replace the ham with sliced leftover sausage or leave it out altogether, and use any cheese you like. All that really matters is that you can form a pie: whatever size tortillas you use, they have to be able to line your dish, and come at least ¾ inch up the sides.

It is not advisable to make ahead/store

SERVES 1–2 (SEE RECIPE INTRODUCTION)

Regular olive oil – 2 teaspoons
Flour tortillas – 2 large
Ham – 1–2 slices (approx. 2 ounces), torn into pieces
Eggs – 2 large, at room temperature
Sea salt flakes or kosher salt – a pinch
Cheddar – ¼ cup, grated
Hot sauce – to taste

1   Preheat the oven to 400°F. Pour 1 teaspoon of the oil into a shallowish, round, ovenproof dish, and use a pastry brush to grease the base and sides lightly. Line it with 1 of the tortillas, making sure it comes up the sides a little. In effect, you are creating a tortilla bowl inside your dish.

2   Drop in the ham, crack in the eggs – sprinkling the yolks with a little salt – and then scatter about a third of your grated cheese on top.

3   Brush one side of the second tortilla with oil – keeping a little bit of oil in reserve – and place it, oiled-side up, loosely on top of the filling. Press the edges of the tortillas together, pushing them down into the dish and up the sides, then brush these edges with a little more oil.

4   Top with the remaining cheese, then add a few squeezes or shakes of hot sauce, depending on how fiery you want this to be. Bake in the oven for 15 minutes, by which time the eggs will be cooked inside, the cheese melted, and the edges of the tortilla crust crisped and browned. Ovens do vary, so you may find you need to alter the cooking time. Eat immediately. This is not a huge problem.

BLACK PUDDING HASH
WITH FRIED EGG

You either hate black pudding (otherwise known as blood sausage or boudin noir) or you love it. And while I wouldn't even try to win over the former, it gives me pleasure to gratify the latter. This is not entirely selfless, since I belong firmly in this camp. Given the choice, I go for Stornoway black pudding, which has a firmer texture and crisps up more as it cooks, but I have yet to meet a black pudding that I don't like, and a softer, moussier-textured version will do just as well. I've given the recipe here assuming you're starting off with uncooked potatoes, which means you need some water in the pan as you cook them, but if you make this with leftover cooked potatoes (of whatever sort) just fry the cubes in oil until crisp.

It is not advisable to make ahead/store

SERVES 2

Regular olive oil – 2 tablespoons, plus 2 tablespoons for the eggs

Potato – 1 large, peeled and cut into 1 inch chunks, to give 2¼ cups loosely packed

Cold water – ¼ cup

Sea salt flakes or kosher salt – ½ teaspoon, plus more to taste

Scallion – 1, thinly sliced

Red chile – 1, seeded and finely chopped

Black pudding – 8 ounces, cut into approx. 1 inch cubes

Eggs – 2 large, at room temperature

1   Heat 2 tablespoons of oil in a medium-sized, heavy-based, non-stick frying pan and fry the cubed potatoes in a single layer, over a high heat, for 5 minutes. Then stir for a further minute, before gently pouring the water over and sprinkling in the salt. Stir again, and once the water has bubbled up, turn the heat down to medium and leave to cook for another 7–10 minutes until the water has evaporated and the potatoes are cooked through.

2   Add most of the scallion and most of the chile, give a good stir for about 30 seconds, then push the potatoes to the edges of the pan, so they form a beautiful golden frame, and tumble the black pudding into the space in the middle. Leave to fry, without touching it, for 2½ minutes, then stir everything together gently in the pan and cook for another minute until the black pudding is hot all the way through.

3   Taste to see if you need more salt, then divide the hash between two waiting plates. Wipe out the pan with some paper towels, making sure not to burn yourself, then add the remaining 2 tablespoons of oil, and when hot, crack in the 2 eggs and fry them, spooning some of the hot oil over, so that the white around the yolk cooks through. Top the hash with the fried eggs, and sprinkle over the remaining scallion and chile.

GOLDEN EGG CURRY

This magnificent addition to my eating life comes courtesy of Yasmin Othman (who has brought much deliciousness my way over the years) and I glow with gratitude every time I eat it. This – called *masak lemak telur* in Malaysian – is very far removed from the egg curries I remember from my early youth, and would much prefer to forget. What we have here are eggs poached in a rich, aromatic, turmeric-tinted, tamarind-sharp, coconutty sauce or soup.

This has definite heat, but not eye-wateringly so. If you'd like it a bit milder, do not pierce the three whole Thai chiles. And if you'd like it a lot milder, then you could seed the Thai chile that goes in the paste, and dispense with the whole ones in the soup. But even if, like me, you love fiery food, I don't advise eating the whole chiles. I won't stop you, but you have been warned.

For make ahead/store notes see p.274

1   With an immersion blender, blitz the jalapeño chiles and 1 roughly chopped green Thai chile, shallots, garlic, ginger, and turmeric to a paste.

2   Heat the oil in a heavy-based wok or a pan of similarly wide diameter that comes with a lid, add the paste and the lemongrass and fry gently, stirring frequently, for 5 minutes, by which time the paste will be cooked and softened. Either don't use a wooden spoon here, or use one you don't mind being stained by the turmeric.

3   Add the coconut milk, water, sea salt, and tamarind. Make a couple of little incisions in each of the 3 whole green Thai chiles with the point of a small sharp knife and drop them in, too. Turn the heat up to bring to a near boil, then reduce the heat again and simmer gently for about 7 minutes, stirring frequently, until the sauce has cooked and reduced to a thick golden soup.

4   Crack the eggs into the sauce (if you're cautious, you could crack each of them into a cup first), cover with a lid, and leave to simmer very gently for about 4 minutes, or until the whites are set but the yolks still runny, or cook for longer if you want well-cooked yolks. You'll have to lift the lid to monitor how the eggs are cooking.

5   Divide between two bowls, trying to spoon out most of the sauce from the pan first. Serve with rice, dippable flatbreads, or both.

SERVES 2

Fresh jalapeño chiles – 2, seeded and roughly chopped
Green Thai chiles – 4 in total, 1 roughly chopped and 3 left whole
Shallots – 5 ounces (approx. 5 small round ones), peeled and roughly chopped
Garlic – 2 fat cloves, peeled and roughly chopped
Fresh ginger – 1½-inch piece, peeled and roughly chopped
Fresh turmeric – 3-inch piece, peeled and roughly chopped, or 1 teaspoon ground turmeric
Vegetable oil – 2 tablespoons
Lemongrass – 1 stalk, trimmed and bruised
Coconut milk – 1 x 14-ounce can
Water from a freshly boiled kettle – 7 tablespoons
Sea salt flakes or kosher salt – 2 teaspoons
Tamarind paste – 2 teaspoons
Eggs – 4 large, at room temperature

To serve:
Rice or flatbreads (or both)

DEVILED EGGS

While deviled eggs are an essential part of the American entertaining tradition, particularly on the Southern table, they have never quite caught on in the UK – though they did have a moment, at least at my grandmother's table – with the same brio, and I'd like to see that change. Actually, and to my shame, I'd all but forgotten about them until I came across a recipe in a favorite book of mine, *Being Dead Is No Excuse: The Official Southern Ladies Guide to Hosting the Perfect Funeral*. There's not much that can get me squeezing a fancy-tipped pastry bag, but this recipe – even if mine diverges somewhat – compelled me to. Although they are a bit fiddly to make, they're not difficult, and they are always a major hit. And I'm talking about genuine enjoyment not ironic amusement. As many as I make, I never have a single one left over.

It's best to use eggs that are approaching their expiration date, as the fresher they are, the harder they are to peel. In order to help keep the yolk centered as the eggs cook, leave them lying on their sides in a dish (rather than sitting upright in their boxes) overnight before cooking them. It's not a fail-safe guarantee, but it does seem to make a difference.

For make ahead/store notes see p.274

For make ahead/store notes see p.274

MAKES 18

Eggs – 12 large, at room temperature (and see last paragraph of recipe introduction)
Mayonnaise – ¼ cup
English or Dijon mustard – 1–2 teaspoons
Sea salt flakes or kosher salt – 1 teaspoon, or more to taste
Paprika – ¼ teaspoon, plus more for sprinkling
Tabasco – a few drops, to taste
Extra-virgin olive oil – 2 tablespoons
Water from a freshly boiled kettle – 2–3 tablespoons
Chives – 2 teaspoons finely chopped

1   Bring some water to a boil in a saucepan that's big enough to hold the 12 eggs on their sides and, once it's boiling, gently ferry the eggs, one by one, into the pan and bring back to a boil. Boil for 1 minute, then turn the heat off and leave the eggs to stand in the pan for 12 minutes.

2   While you're waiting for the eggs to cook, fill a large bowl with very cold water, and throw in a handful of ice cubes if you have them. As soon as the eggs have had their 12 minutes, spoon them, egg by egg, into the cold water and leave for 15 minutes – no longer – before peeling patiently and carefully.

3   Halve the eggs lengthwise and, using your fingers, gently prise the yolk out of each half and put them into a mixing bowl. Place the neatest looking 18 halved whites on a plate or two. You need more yolk than white, as it were, to fill each egg.

4   To the bowl, add the mayonnaise, a teaspoon of English mustard, the salt and paprika, and shake a few drops of Tabasco

on top. Stir and mash with a fork, then blitz to mix with an immersion blender. Add the oil and blitz again until smooth. It will be very thick. Check for seasoning and also taste to see if you want this hotter. I generally go up to 2 teaspoons of mustard and quite a bit more Tabasco, but it's best to proceed slowly. Now, by hand, stir in as much of the water as you need to help form a piping consistency.

5   Fit a pastry bag with a star tip and spoon in the golden mixture, making sure it is densely packed at the bottom of the bag. Then pipe away, filling the hollowed-out whites with golden rosettes. Or you can mound the yolk mixture using a pair of teaspoons. Sprinkle with paprika and chopped chives and serve with a flourish.

TOMATO AND FRIED BREAD HASH

When I was at university, fried bread with canned tomatoes was the Friday breakfast special in the college canteen. While I have no bad word to say against the "fried slice" – one of Britain's great contributions to culinary culture, sadly now out of favor – its pairing with canned tomatoes always worried me.

This jumbled version, unlike the original, needs to be made with good – rather than pre-sliced, pappy plastic – bread. And please don't get agitated about the amount of oil: most of it is poured away once the bread cubes have been fried, and these in turn are not greasy, but resoundingly crunchy.

An excellent sop for excess alcohol, this is as good for a late supper as it is for breakfast. I like to have a bottle of Worcestershire sauce (already essential in the hash) on the table alongside, but no one would argue with you if you chose to shake a few drops of Tabasco over it while you eat.

It is not advisable to make ahead/store

1   Line a plate with a couple of pieces of paper towel, and sit it near the stove. Heat the oil in a heavy-based wok or frying pan: you can test whether it's hot enough by dropping in one of the cubes of bread; if it makes the oil sizzle, you're ready to go. Equally, if the bread darkens straightaway, you'll need to take the wok off the heat for a bit to cool the oil down.

2   Carefully tumble the cubes of bread into the hot oil and fry – stirring as needed to get them crisp on all sides – for a bare minute, or until you have gorgeously golden to golden-brown croutons. Transfer them to the paper-lined plate, then discard most of the oil, leaving about 2 tablespoonfuls in the wok.

3   Turn the heat down, then add the shallot, sprinkle with salt, and cook, stirring frequently, for around 5 minutes until softened and slightly caramelized around the edges, then stir in the minced garlic.

4   Now turn the heat up, then add the tomatoes and cook, stirring, until the pulpy interior has collapsed a little and the skins have softened. Frankly, I'd be amazed if this took more than a couple of minutes.

5   Add the Worcestershire sauce, grind in some pepper, generously, sprinkle in about half of the chopped chives and give a quick stir,

SERVES 2

Regular olive oil – 7 tablespoons
Bread – 2–3 thick slices, crusts removed and cut into cubes
Shallot – 1 large (approx. 2 ounces), peeled and cut into fine-ish half-moons
Sea salt flakes or kosher salt – a generous pinch
Garlic – 1 fat clove, peeled and minced
Tomatoes – 3 medium-large (approx. 12 ounces), cut into chunks
Worcestershire sauce – 2 teaspoons
Pepper – a good grinding
Chives – 2 tablespoons finely chopped

before returning the crisp, cooked cubes of bread to the pan. Toss everything together in a sprightly fashion, then divide between two waiting plates. Sprinkle with the rest of the chives, and dive in.

CHILI CHEESE GARLIC BREAD

Garlic bread – a damp-centered, often bendy, stick of it – was a dominating feature of my eating life in the '70s and '80s. This is a more robust version, gooey with cheese and warmly, rather than fierily, flecked with crushed red pepper flakes.

For make ahead/store notes see p.274

For make ahead/store notes see p.274

1   Preheat the oven to 425°F.

2   Beat together the butter, salt, garlic, and red pepper flakes, then duly beat in the mozzarella.

3   Cut the bread on the diagonal into slices approximately 1 inch apart, taking care not to go all the way through to the bottom.

4   Spread the garlic butter mixture generously and evenly between the slices, and then smear the last scrapings down the middle of the top of the loaf.

5   Wrap the bread in aluminum foil with a fold at the top so that it can be opened easily, and bake for 30 minutes. Open the parcel carefully; if the bread is still soft on top, put it back in the oven, with the foil pulled back a little, and cook for another 5 minutes until the top is crisp. Remove from the oven, lift the bread out of the foil (without burning your fingers) and place the crisp bread on a board. Using a large serrated knife, cut through to separate the slices.

MAKES APPROX. 10 SLICES, DEPENDING ON THE DIMENSIONS OF THE LOAF

Unsalted butter – 7 tablespoons, soft
Sea salt flakes or kosher salt – ½ teaspoon
Garlic – 4 fat cloves, peeled and minced
Crushed red pepper flakes – ⅛ teaspoon
Fresh mozzarella – 4 ounces, well drained, and finely chopped, to give 1 cup loosely packed
Small white sourdough loaf or other good chewy bread – approx. 14 ounces

WHIPPED FETA TOASTS

MAKES APPROX. 8 TOASTS,
DEPENDING ON THE SIZE OF
THE LOAF

Feta cheese – 4 ounces, at room
temperature, crumbled, to give 1 cup
loosely packed

Plain whole milk Greek yogurt –
¼ cup, at room temperature

Ground cumin – ¼ teaspoon

Lemon – 1, finely grated zest

Honey – 1 teaspoon

Extra-virgin olive oil – 2 teaspoons

Sea salt flakes or kosher salt –
to taste

Sourdough or other good bread –
approx. 8 slices (see recipe introduction),
toasted and cooled a little

Topping of your choice (see
recipe introduction)

Drizzled with a little extra honey and topped with toasted pine nuts, these make a wonderful, gently exotic breakfast. Topped with thin-as-you-can slices of cucumber and radish and feathery dill, they're an excellent lightish lunch or cocktail time bite. But why stop there? You can really add whatever combination of ingredients you want. Think griddled zucchini tongues with a sprinkle of sumac, or roasted red peppers with capers, simply flecked with *pul biber* (aka Turkish red pepper flakes or Aleppo pepper), or – go crazy – chopped strawberry and mint.

While you can whip the feta without an electric hand mixer, just know you will have a thicker, less smooth mixture to play with, which means it won't go as far. And you will need to go at it fairly vigorously for a good while by hand.

It's difficult to say exactly how many toasts you'll get out of this. It depends on the dimensions of the loaf you're using, and how thickly or thinly you want to spread the whipped feta. The number of slices I suggest is based on using a fairly squat, small sourdough. And if it helps, know that you can expect to have about ¾ cup of whipped feta to play with.

For make ahead/store notes see p.274

1   Crumble the feta into a medium-sized bowl, add the yogurt, cumin, lemon zest, honey, and oil and beat together with a spatula or wooden spoon, then whip with an electric hand mixer till creamy. You're unlikely to need to add much salt, if any, but taste and see how you feel.

2   When the toast has cooled, spread generously with the whipped feta, slice in half if wished and top as desired.

TOASTED BRIE, PROSCIUTTO, AND FIG SANDWICH

Insomnia has its benefits: inspiration for this sandwich came to me in the otherwise fretful small hours. I dare say that, to keep the ingredients more geo-culinarily aligned, the cheese should be Taleggio, Fontina, or even mozzarella, but Brie (un-chic as cooking with it is) it has to be for me.

This sort of food is more an idea than a recipe, by which I mean it's difficult to give exact measurements. It rather depends on the size of bread – which needs to be cut generously, but not so thickly that the heat won't get through the bread to melt the cheese – as well as the size of the fig, and so on.

It is not advisable to make ahead/store

SERVES 1 VERY LUCKY PERSON

Good white bread – 2 slices cut from a loaf, not too thick
Ripe Brie – enough to spread generously on each slice of bread
Pepper – a few grindings
Ripe black fig – 1
Prosciutto – 2–3 slices
Unsalted butter – 4 teaspoons
Vegetable oil – 1 teaspoon

1   Spread the 2 slices of bread with the Brie and grind some pepper on top.

2   Cut the stalk off the fig and discard, then cut off the other end: do not discard, just eat. Slice the fig and arrange on one of the Brie-spread pieces of bread, and drape the other piece with prosciutto and sandwich together.

3   Heat half the butter and half the oil in a cast iron or other heavy-based, non-stick frying pan in which the sandwich will fit fairly snugly. When foamy, add the sandwich to the pan, and cook over a medium-low heat, gently pressing down on it every now and again with a large cranked spatula, or tool of your choice, for about 3 minutes, or until the bread is golden brown underneath and the cheese is beginning to ooze a little. Turn the heat down if the butter looks like it's beginning to burn.

4   Add the remaining butter and oil, then straightaway lift the sandwich up with your spatula and flip it over to cook the other side exactly as before, though 2 minutes on this side may well be enough.

5   Remove to a waiting plate, cut in half and enjoy each crisp, gooey, sweet and salty bite.

CATALAN TOASTS

MAKES APPROX. 6 PIECES,
DEPENDING ON THE SIZE
OF THE LOAF

Very ripe tomato – 1 large but not
beefsteak (approx. 6 ounces), seeded
and very, very finely chopped
Garlic – 1 clove, peeled and minced
Extra-virgin olive oil – 1 tablespoon
Sourdough or other rustic bread –
approx. 3 chunky slices, halved
Sea salt flakes or kosher salt –
to taste

I first came across these in a tapas bar in Barcelona about 100 years ago. *Pa amb tomàquet* in Catalan, they are, I suppose, a version of an Italian tomato bruschetta, but instead of having roughly chopped tomatoes tumbled onto the bread, here the tomatoes are finely chopped to a fuzzy mush with which the bread is merely anointed. My knife skills are non-existent, so I find it easier to chop the tomatoes into submission with a mezzaluna. You want them practically pulverized.

For make ahead/store notes see p.274

1   Having chopped your tomato very, very finely, keep it on the board. Add the minced garlic, and combine using a fork to crush and mash them, before transferring to a small bowl. Add the oil and fork together so you have a fuzzy light-red mush. Out of this 1 tomato, I get ½ cup of tomato topping. Ideally, leave the tomato mixture covered in plastic wrap for a while, until the tomatoes start exuding their liquid; the toasts are better when they are slightly dampened with the tomato topping.

2   Toast the bread – I like mine well-toasted and charred at the edges – halving the slices if wished, then spread modestly with the tomato mixture; the bread should still be visible under the scant topping. Sprinkle with salt.

PARMESAN FRENCH TOAST

While obviously a contender for weekend brunch, this savory take on French toast is, for me, a perfect early supper when I feel like something comforting and quick. It's also exactly what I need when I've come back in late, having uncharacteristically and disturbingly gone without dinner.

The white sourdough bread I keep in the house is a modest-sized loaf. If you happen to have a huge loaf of bread use just one slice and halve it.

It is not advisable to make ahead/store

1   Whisk the egg, Parmesan, paprika, mustard, Worcestershire sauce, and milk together in a shallow dish that the slices of bread will fit in with not a great deal of space around them, making sure everything is completely combined.

2   Sit the bread in this sunny mixture for about 2 minutes each side, pressing down on it every now and again. You want the slices to be soaked through and softened, but not falling to pieces. Spoon any remaining egg mixture over.

3   When the bread is ready, warm the butter and oil in a frying pan in which the slices will sit fairly snugly. Once the butter is beginning to bubble frothily, fry the bread over a medium-high heat, turning it down if the butter gets too hot, for about 2 minutes each side – keep a good eye on it – until it is cooked through with patches of rich golden brown on the surface.

4   Remove from the pan, and eat just as it is, or sprinkle with chopped parsley and thinly sliced scallion, if wished.

SERVES 1–2

Egg – 1 large
Parmesan – 3 tablespoons finely grated
Paprika – ¼ teaspoon
Dijon mustard – 1 teaspoon
Worcestershire sauce – ½ teaspoon
Whole milk – 3 tablespoons
White sourdough bread or anything sturdy and with a bit of bite to it – 2 slices, not too thick (see recipe introduction)
Unsalted butter – 1 tablespoon
Regular olive oil – ½ teaspoon

To serve:
Italian parsley
Scallion

BEEF AND EGGPLANT FATTEH

This is a subtly textured, richly flavored arrangement of toasted pieces of flatbread topped with meaty eggplant and beef, a garlicky tahini-yogurt sauce, red pepper flakes, pomegranate seeds, toasted pine nuts, and fresh shredded mint. I think of this rather as a refined, Middle Eastern form of nachos.

For make ahead/store notes see p.274

1   Preheat the oven to 400°F. Spread the pita triangles out onto a large baking sheet and toast for 10–15 minutes, or until they are crisp. You don't need them to color, but if they do just a little here and there, that's not a bad thing. Set the pita triangles aside for the moment.

2   Beat the yogurt, tahini, lemon juice, garlic, and 1 teaspoon of salt together in a heatproof bowl that will later sit over a saucepan. Taste to see if you want any more salt. Put to one side while you cook the eggplant-beef layer.

3   Warm the oil in a wide, though not deep, heavy-based saucepan or Dutch oven and cook the onion, stirring occasionally, over a medium-low heat for 5 minutes, then turn the heat down to low and carry on cooking it, still stirring occasionally, until soft and a pale caramel color. This will take another 4 minutes or so.

4   Turn the heat up to medium, tumble in the eggplant cubes, and stir well to mix with the onion. Stay by the stove as you will need to stir frequently, and cook them for about 10 minutes. Turn the heat down if they look as if they're catching.

5   Stir in the cumin, coriander, and a teaspoon each of Aleppo pepper and salt and, now over a high heat, add the beef and use a fork to break it up a little and turn in the pan until it's lost its red color. Turn the heat back down to medium and cook for 10 minutes, stirring occasionally, until the meat is cooked through. Taste to see if you want to add more salt, then take off the heat while you return to the tahini-yogurt sauce.

6   Pour some just-boiled water into a fresh saucepan, enough to come about 1¼ inches up the sides, and put over a low heat. Sit the bowl with the tahini-yogurt mixture on top, making sure the bowl does

SERVES 4–6

For the base:
Pita breads – 4 (approx. 9 ounces), split open and cut into nacho-sized triangles

For the topping:
Plain whole milk Greek yogurt – 2 cups
Tahini – 5 tablespoons, at room temperature
Lemon – 1–2, to give 3 tablespoons of juice
Garlic – 2 cloves, peeled and minced
Sea salt flakes or kosher salt – 1–2 teaspoons, to taste

For the eggplant-beef layer:
Regular olive oil – 3 tablespoons
Onion – 1 small, peeled and finely chopped, to give heaping ¾ cup loosely packed
Eggplant – 1 medium-large, cut into small cubes, to give 3⅔ cups loosely packed
Ground cumin – 2 teaspoons
Ground coriander – 2 teaspoons
Aleppo pepper (see p.14) or paprika – 1 teaspoon, plus more for sprinkling
Sea salt flakes or kosher salt – 1–2 teaspoons, to taste
Ground beef – 1 pound

To sprinkle over:
Pomegranate seeds – heaping ¾ cup loosely packed
Pine nuts – ⅓ cup, toasted
Mint – 1 tablespoon finely shredded leaves

not touch the water. Beat well until the yogurt is slightly above room temperature and has the consistency of lightly whipped cream.

7   Now for the grand assembly: arrange the crisp pita triangles on a large round plate (I use one of about 12 inches in diameter). Top with the eggplant-beef mixture, followed by the yogurt-tahini sauce. Sprinkle with the Aleppo pepper (or paprika, if you're using that) to give a light dusting. Scatter over the pomegranate seeds and toasted pine nuts and, finally, strew with the finely shredded mint leaves. Eat with your fingers, nacho-style.

SPELT SPAGHETTI WITH SPICY SESAME MUSHROOMS

Whole wheat pasta holds no charm for me, but I co-exist very amicably with spelt spaghetti. Here it acts as a rather more robust form of soba noodle, which makes perfect sense since the sauce that dresses the pasta is Asian-influenced rather than Italian. In this vein, leftovers make an instant noodle salad.

For make ahead/store notes see p.274

1   Put a large saucepan of water on to heat for the spaghetti. When it's almost come to a boil, get started on the sauce.

2   Warm the vegetable oil in a wide, deep frying pan (large enough to take the pasta later) that has a lid and add the finely chopped scallions, stirring for a minute until they become vibrantly green.

3   Add the sliced mushrooms and cook them for 3–4 minutes over a medium-high heat, turning them frequently in the pan.

4   Add the sesame seeds, the minced garlic, soy sauce, sesame oil, red pepper flakes, zest of ½ the lemon, and the tablespoon of juice and stir everything together, then clamp on the lid and leave on a low heat to simmer for another 5 minutes, until the mushrooms are soft.

5   Once the pasta water's boiling, salt exuberantly and cook the spaghetti, using the timing on the package as a guide, but start testing a few minutes before. If your mushrooms are ready while the pasta's still cooking, just turn off the heat and leave the pan as it is on the stove.

6   Using a pasta claw or tongs, lift the cooked spaghetti straight into the pan of mushrooms and toss together with most of the chopped parsley. Or drain the pasta, reserving some of the cooking water first. Add a little of the pasta water to help sauce and spaghetti cohere. Go spoonful by spoonful; you may not need much.

7   Divide into bowls and sprinkle with the last bit of chopped parsley.

SERVES 2–3

Vegetable oil – 1 tablespoon
Scallions – 4, finely chopped
Crimini mushrooms – 10 ounces, sliced, to give 3¾ cups loosely packed
Sesame seeds – 2 teaspoons
Garlic – 2 cloves, peeled and minced
Soy sauce – 2 tablespoons
Asian sesame oil – 2 teaspoons
Crushed red pepper flakes – ¼ teaspoon
Lemon – finely grated zest of ½, plus 1 tablespoon of juice
Salt – for pasta water
Spelt spaghetti – 8 ounces
Italian parsley – leaves from a small bunch, finely chopped, to give 1 cup loosely packed

GEMELLI WITH ANCHOVIES, TOMATOES, AND MASCARPONE

SERVES 2

Gemelli pasta – 6 ounces
Salt – for pasta water
Regular olive oil – 1 tablespoon
Anchovy fillets – 6, finely chopped
Garlic – 1 clove, peeled and minced
Crushed red pepper flakes –
¼ teaspoon
Cherry or grape tomatoes –
6 ounces (1 cup), halved across the
equator
Dry white vermouth – ¼ cup
Mascarpone – 2 tablespoons
Parmesan – 1 tablespoon finely grated,
plus more to serve
Italian parsley – 2 tablespoons finely
chopped leaves, plus more to serve

Quick, simple and – much as I hate the word – tasty. I know no self-respecting Italian would let tomato seeds sully a sauce, but I do so very happily, and it's the gloop inside the halved cherry tomatoes that adds cohesion to the spicy, tangy creaminess.

Gemelli – which means twins in Italian – are a robust short pasta shape, formed out of what looks like two sturdy strings twisted together but are in fact made out of a single rope of pasta, doubled back on itself like a helicoidal twist. If you can't find them – though they're very much worth seeking out – then substitute casarecce or, easier still, fusilli.

It is not advisable to make ahead/store

1   Put a saucepan of water on to boil for the pasta. (Although you don't need to start cooking your sauce till the pasta's in, I'd get everything ready for it while you wait.) Once it's come to a boil, salt generously and add the pasta. Check the pasta package for advised cooking times, but do start tasting a good 2 minutes before you're told it should be ready.

2   Once the pasta is in, put the oil and finely chopped anchovies into a heavy-based wok, or other capacious pan, and cook, stirring over a medium heat for about a minute, or until the anchovies have almost dissolved into the oil. Stir in the garlic and red pepper flakes, then turn the heat up a little and tumble in the tomatoes, stirring them gently for about 2 minutes, or until they are beginning to soften.

3   Pour in the vermouth, let it bubble up, then stir and push the tomatoes about in the pan for around another 2 minutes until they have broken down a little in the thickened, reduced, now orange-tinted liquid. Take the pan off the heat, stir in the mascarpone and, when it's all melted into the sauce, duly stir in the Parmesan and parsley.

4   Before you drain the pasta, lower in a cup to remove some of the cooking water. Or use a mesh ladle or pasta claw to transfer the gemelli directly. Add a tablespoon or so of the cooking water to the pasta sauce; this will help the sauce coat the pasta. Drain the pasta, add it to the sauce and toss well to mix, adding more of the pasta cooking water if needed. Sprinkle with a little parsley and take the Parmesan to the table to serve.

MUSSELS WITH PASTA AND TOMATOES

This is really a rich, red *moules marinière* type of arrangement, studded with short, stubby pasta, rather than a traditional dish of pasta with mussels. Feel free to eat it how you want, of course, but for me it's all about picking the golden flesh from the mussels then greedily spooning up the pasta and sweet, briny, and winey juices. When I make this for two, I keep the mussels as they are but halve the amount of pasta. If you can't find ditalini by all means use macaroni.

It is not advisable to make ahead/store

1   Clean the beards from the mussels, rubbing any other debris off their shells as well, and leave them to soak in a bowl of cold water while you get on with everything else.

2   Put a saucepan of water on to boil for the pasta, and once it has come to a boil, salt the water and cook the ditalini following the package instructions, checking 2 minutes before time's up, just in case they are cooked: you don't want the pasta too soft.

3   While the pasta is cooking, heat the oil in a wide saucepan (I use one of 11 inches diameter) that has a lid, and that can take the pasta and mussels later. Tumble in the halved tomatoes and cook for a couple of minutes over a medium-high heat, stirring frequently, to soften.

4   Stir in the garlic, red pepper flakes, and salt, and then keep stirring frequently until the tomatoes start to melt down and make juice. This won't take very long. Pour in the vermouth, let it bubble up and then give everything a good stir.

5   Drain the mussels, discarding any that remain open, and tip them into the pan with the tomatoes. Clamp on the lid and let them cook over a medium-high heat for 2–4 minutes – giving the pan the odd shake – until the mussels have opened and added their rich liquor to the pan. If your pan is not that wide, you will have to be more assiduous about shaking, and give a good stir from time to time. Discard any mussels that have stayed closed.

6   Once the pasta is cooked al dente, lift it straight out of the pan with a mesh ladle or slotted spoon and into the pan of mussels, then spoon in 2 tablespoonfuls of the pasta cooking water. Give a good stir, clamp on the lid and leave for a minute or so off the heat.

SERVES 4

Mussels – 2 pounds

Salt – for pasta water

Ditalini rigati pasta – 8 ounces

Regular olive oil – 2 tablespoons

Cherry or grape tomatoes – 8 ounces (1⅓ cups), halved across the equator

Garlic – 2 cloves, peeled and minced

Crushed red pepper flakes – ¼ teaspoon

Sea salt flakes or kosher salt – ½ teaspoon

Red vermouth – ⅓ cup

Italian parsley – ¼ cup roughly chopped leaves

7   Uncover, and stir in most of the parsley, then sprinkle the rest on top. Remember to take a couple of bowls for the detritus to the table, along with the bowls you're eating out of.

CAPELLINI WITH SCALLOPS

I love the delicate silkiness of string-thin capellini, but you do need to act fast when you cook with it, as the fine strands can overcook all too easily. I take my wok with the scallops, once they're cooked, over to sit by the sink, so that I can mix sauce and capellini immediately after the pasta's drained. And life is made very much easier, too, if you have one of those pasta pots with an insert. Obviously, if you're using one of these sorts of pots, you don't need to take the ½ cupful of pasta cooking liquid out before draining, as it will be waiting for you in the pot.

Capellini take around 2 minutes to cook, which is why I make the sauce first. Should you have to use spaghetti or other longer-cooking pasta then start on the sauce when there's about 4 minutes' cooking time left for the pasta.

I think you need a little fire with the tender sweetness of the scallops, so I don't seed the chile. If you wish to, though, be my guest.

More euphoniously, in Italian this is *capellini con le cappesante*.

It is not advisable to make ahead/store

SERVES 2–3

Regular olive oil – 2 tablespoons
Red chile – 1, finely chopped
Garlic – 1 clove, peeled and minced
Italian parsley – ¼ cup finely chopped leaves
Sea scallops, coral-less – 6 ounces, cut into small dice
Sea salt flakes or kosher salt – ½ teaspoon
Dry white vermouth – ¼ cup
Salt – for pasta water
Capellini pasta – 6 ounces
Extra-virgin olive oil – 1 tablespoon, plus more to serve

1   Put a copious amount of water on to boil in a large saucepan, then put a colander in the sink and get out a serving bowl or bowls now.

2   Once the water is more or less boiling, warm the regular olive oil in a heavy-based wok (or a pan large enough that you can tip the pasta into later) and add the chopped chile, letting it fry for about 30 seconds. Stir in the minced garlic, followed by a couple of tablespoons or so of the chopped parsley. Add the diced scallops and cook, stirring, until they have just lost their glassiness. The red of the chile, green of the parsley, and white of the scallops give you, very pleasingly, the colors of the Italian flag. Add the salt and pour in the vermouth, let it bubble up for ½–1 minute, then take the wok off the heat and move it over to the sink (not in it, obviously).

3   Once the water's boiling vociferously, add salt, then tip in the capellini and cook till al dente, testing frequently. The pasta, in my experience, tends to be ready well before package instructions suggest.

4   When it's nearly ready, remove a ladleful of the cooking water and, when just cooked, carry the pan carefully to the sink, then drain the pasta swiftly and tip it into the nearby wok. Toss well, then add a tablespoon – or more if needed – of the reserved pasta cooking water and the extra-virgin olive oil and toss again, then do likewise with the remaining parsley, leaving a little to sprinkle on top as you serve. Take the extra-virgin olive oil to the table so people can drizzle a little over their own bowls of pasta as they eat.

RADIATORI WITH SAUSAGE AND SAFFRON

The first time I rapturously ate this sauce, it had been cooked for me by one Caz Hildebrand, who is not only the designer of this book and all my previous ones, but also co-author of *The Geometry of Pasta*, from which the recipe is adapted. It's a relatively recent addition to my table, but I feel as if it's belonged on it forever. Simple to make, and enormously comforting, it has a sprightly elegance of flavor. The saffron sings out clearly, and – this initially surprised me – is not remotely overwhelmed by the spice of the Italian sausage.

I realize, though, that the starting point of *The Geometry of Pasta* is the very necessity of matching the right sauce to the shape of pasta, and what am I doing here? Using the wrong pasta. Classically, this is, or should be, *malloreddus alla Campidanese*, and those who don't make their own malloreddus (which look like tiny ridged conch shells or, actually, little grubs) can use gnocchi sardi from a packet. Much as I enjoy the trad pairing, I just happen to love this rich sauce with chunky radiatori – its name rather indicates its form – though the ubiquitous fusilli would not seem an utterly catastrophic choice to me, either. I apologize to all offended Sardinians. And, no doubt to the dismay of Italians everywhere, I do have to say it's also very good over polenta.

Now, I've written the recipe here as if making and eating the sauce on the same day. Actually, I think it's very much better made in advance and left to mellow in the fridge, in which case you won't need to be putting the pasta water on, and so forth, while you're making the sauce. I also very often make this quantity of sauce and freeze half. Indeed, I wouldn't want my freezer ever to be without it.

For make ahead/store notes see p.274

For make ahead/store notes see p.274

SERVES 4–6

For the sauce:
Regular olive oil – 3 tablespoons
Onion – 1 large, peeled and roughly chopped, to give 1⅓ cups loosely packed
Sea salt flakes or kosher salt – a pinch
Italian sausage – 1 pound, squeezed out of the skins
Saffron threads – ¼ teaspoon
Tomato passata or tomato sauce – 2½ cups

Radiatori pasta – 1 pound
Salt – for pasta water

To serve:
Basil
Pecorino – to grate over (otherwise use Parmesan if wished)

1   Warm the oil in a capacious heavy-based Dutch oven or saucepan, large enough to take both sauce and pasta later if possible. Add the chopped onion, turn it in the oil, sprinkle the salt over and cook over a medium-low heat, stirring every now and again, until softened, which will take around 10 minutes.

2   Turn the heat up a bit, add the sausage meat, breaking it up with a fork, and stirring it in the pan until it begins to lose its raw color – about 5 minutes – and then add the saffron and tomato passata. Give a good stir, then once it's begun to bubble, turn the heat down low (moving it across to a smaller burner on the stove if

necessary) and leave to cook at a very gentle simmer for 40 minutes. Keep an eye on it, to make sure it's not cooking too quickly.

3   You can cook the pasta when the sauce is almost ready or, which is probably easier, turn the heat off under the pan of sauce, and clamp on a lid and let it stand waiting for the pasta.

4   So, when the pasta water's boiling, salt it well, then add the pasta, and cook following the package instructions, although start checking 2 minutes before it says it will be ready. Just before you drain the pasta, reserve a couple of ladlefuls of the pasta cooking water.

5   Tip the drained pasta into the pan of sauce, and toss together, adding as much pasta cooking water as you need to help everything amalgamate. Serve sprinkled with basil and – preferably – Pecorino to grate over.

MEATBALLS WITH ORZO

Orzo pasta is a non-negotiable staple in my kitchen. Simply dressed in butter and salt, and maybe a dusting of nutmeg or grated Parmesan, or indeed both, it often serves at my table as a substitute for rice or potatoes, and I regularly use it to cook what in Italian is *pasta risottata*, a kind of pasta risotto. It makes for wonderful, cozy one-pot dishes, of which this is a preeminent example.

For make ahead/store notes see p.274

1   Line a large baking sheet with plastic wrap, then put all the ingredients for the meatballs into a large bowl and mix together, gently, with your hands. Don't overmix, as it will make the meatballs dense-textured and heavy.

2   Pinch out pieces of this mixture and roll between the palms of your hand to form meatballs that are somewhere between a cherry tomato and a walnut in size, putting them on your lined sheet as you go. You should get about 30 meatballs.

3   Fill a measuring jug with 4 cups of cold water and put near the stove.

4   Heat the oil in a heavy-based Dutch oven or saucepan that comes with a lid and is large enough to take the meatballs and pasta, too. Cook the chopped onion over a medium heat, stirring every now and again, for about 10 minutes, or until completely softened, then stir in the parsley and oregano and cook, stirring for a minute or so before adding the vermouth. Let this bubble up for a minute and then tip in the tomatoes. Half-fill the empty cans with water from the measuring jug you have at the ready, give them a good swill, and pour into the pan, along with the rest of the water and the salt. Bring to a boil, turn the heat down, clamp on the lid and leave to simmer gently for 10 minutes.

5   Uncover the pan and drop the meatballs gently into the simmering sauce. I try to let these fall in concentric circles, working around the pan from the outside edge inwards, but this is more habit than necessity. Bring it back up to a boil, then turn the heat down again, put the lid back on and simmer the meatballs for 20 minutes. Remove the lid, tip in the orzo, stir gently and turn up the heat to bring back to a bubble. Cook at a robust simmer for 10–15 minutes, or until the pasta is cooked. You will have to give the odd gentle

SERVES 4–6

For the meatballs:
Ground beef – 1 pound
Egg – 1 large, lightly beaten
Italian parsley – 3 tablespoons finely chopped leaves, plus more to serve
Dried bread crumbs – 2 tablespoons
Parmesan – ¼ cup finely grated, plus more to serve
Sea salt flakes or kosher salt – 1½ teaspoons
Garlic – 2 cloves, peeled and minced

For the sauce:
Cold water – 4 cups
Regular olive oil – 2 tablespoons
Onion – 1, peeled and finely chopped, to give 1 cup loosely packed
Italian parsley – 2 tablespoons finely chopped leaves
Dried oregano – 2 teaspoons
Red vermouth – ¼ cup
Canned diced tomatoes – 2 x 14-ounce cans
Sea salt flakes or kosher salt – 1½ teaspoons

Orzo pasta – 10 ounces (1½ cups)

stir throughout this time to make sure the orzo isn't sticking to the bottom of the pan.

6 Serve in shallow bowls, sprinkled with parsley, and with Parmesan on the table alongside.

MUNG BEAN DAL
WITH MINT AND CILANTRO RAITA

These tiny, vibrantly khaki (if that's not too strange a concept) beans, thickened with red lentils, make for a dal with a mild and modest, earthy simplicity; the herbed yogurt and turmeric rice turn it into a meatless feast. But even if you're not going all out and making the rice to go with it, it does need its green yogurt sauce. And while I much prefer the richness of coconut-milk yogurt here (which, for interested parties, does keep it vegan), it can also be made with plain whole milk Greek yogurt.

For make ahead/store notes see p.274

1   Soak the mung beans in enough cold water to cover for at least an hour and up to six, then drain and put them into a heavy Dutch oven or heavy-based saucepan that has a lid.

2   Add the red lentils and the 6 cups of cold water and bring to a boil, leaving the pot uncovered. As the beans come to a boil, skim off the foam on top as best you can. Don't go crazy here: it's impossible to remove all of it (and intensely boring).

3   Now add the chopped red chiles, minced garlic, and turmeric and give the pot a good stir, then simmer partially covered for 30–40 minutes. Take a look at it every now and again: don't let the simmer become too enthusiastic, and stir occasionally. Once the beans and lentils are soft, remove the lid and carry on cooking, uncovered, until you have a rich but still soupy consistency. This will probably take about 10 more minutes depending on how much liquid you have left in the pan at this stage; indeed you may not even need this last step. And bear in mind that the dal will thicken as it stands. Season to taste with the salt.

4   To make the raita, which can easily be whipped up as the dal stands, put the yogurt, cilantro, mint, and salt into a bowl and, with an immersion blender, blitz together. Serve with Turmeric Rice, p.59, if wished.

SERVES 4–6

For the dal:
Dried mung beans – 1¼ cups
Red lentils – ½ cup
Cold water – 6 cups
Red chiles – 2, seeded and finely chopped
Garlic – 1 clove, peeled and minced
Ground turmeric – ½ teaspoon
Sea salt flakes or kosher salt – 1–2 teaspoons, to taste

For the mint and cilantro raita:
Coconut-milk yogurt – 1 cup
Cilantro – leaves from a small bunch, to give 1 cup loosely packed
Mint – ¼ cup very roughly chopped leaves
Sea salt flakes or kosher salt – ½ teaspoon

To serve:
Turmeric Rice with Cardamom and Cumin (see p.59)

TURMERIC RICE
WITH CARDAMOM AND CUMIN

SERVES 4–6

Basmati rice – 1¾ cups

Sea salt flakes or

kosher salt – 1 teaspoon

Ground turmeric – ¼ teaspoon

Cardamom pods – 4, cracked

Cumin seeds – 1 teaspoon

Water from a freshly boiled

kettle – 3 cups

Without doubt, the best way of cooking rice if you want exquisitely separated grains is to use a rice cooker. But my way of approximating this is to leave the rice, once cooked, covered with a tea towel and the lid clamped back on top of the pan, for 40 minutes. True, the rice won't be piping hot, but I don't mind that. It is the standing time that helps banish clumpiness and fluff this golden, glorious-scented rice up further. But if you want your rice hotter, or haven't got the time to wait, then let's settle on 20 minutes.

For make ahead/store notes see p.275

1   Put the rice into a wide, heavy-based pot – enamelled cast iron if you possibly can – with an equally sturdy, well-fitting lid. Tip in the salt, ground turmeric, cardamom pods, and cumin seeds and stir to combine.

2   With the pot over a high heat, add the boiling water and stir again. Once the pot has come up to a boil, clamp on the lid, turn the heat down to as low as possible (moving it to a smaller ring if necessary), and let it cook for 20 minutes, at a very gentle simmer. Don't be tempted to peek before then, as it will let out the steam the rice is cooking in.

3   Check the rice at 20 minutes, by which time the water should have been absorbed and the rice should be cooked through and no longer chalky.

4   Take off the lid, fluff the rice with a fork, cover the pot with a clean tea towel, clamp the lid back on and let the rice stand off the heat for at least 20 and up to 40 minutes before serving.

CARROTS AND FENNEL WITH HARISSA

This has perfectly balanced oomph: the sweetness of the carrots, that particular herbal freshness of fennel, the mellow citrus tang of clementine (though the zest of half an orange, along with 2 tablespoons of juice, would do), and the aromatic heat of harissa.

For make ahead/store notes see p.275

1   Preheat the oven to 350°F.

2   Put the prepared carrots and fennel into a large bowl. Add the harissa, oil, clementine zest and juice, and teaspoon of salt and toss well to combine.

3   Tip into a shallow roasting pan, scraping out the bowl well, give a final toss to mix, spread out in the pan and roast for 40–50 minutes – giving a stir after 30 – until the carrot is just cooked through and the fennel soft. Taste, and add more salt (or not) as desired.

SERVES 4–6

Carrots – 1 pound, peeled and cut into approx. 1½ inch long batons
Fennel – 1 pound, trimmed, halved from top to bottom, then cut into approx. ½-inch-thick slices
Harissa – 2 tablespoons
Regular olive oil – 2 tablespoons
Clementine – 1, finely grated zest, plus 2 tablespoons of juice
Sea salt flakes or kosher salt – 1 teaspoon, or to taste

ROASTED RED ENDIVE

SERVES 3–4

Red endive – 1 pound (4–5 heads), quartered
Sea salt flakes or kosher salt – 1 teaspoon
Regular olive oil – ¼ cup
Dry white vermouth – ⅓ cup
Thyme – a few sprigs

If you're of the bitter-is-better school of eating – which I emphatically am – then this is for you. I think there isn't a week that goes past when I don't cook this, and I often make it just to let it get cold and eat it as a salad whenever I feel the urge. But even if you are hesitant about bitterness, this may still be for you: the oven mellows the rasping bite of the raw endive and, for reasons I don't quite understand, the dry white vermouth makes it sweeten as it cooks.

For make ahead/store notes see p.275

1   Preheat the oven to 400°F. Arrange the quartered endive spears, cut-side up, in a shallow roasting pan in which they sit snugly. Sprinkle with salt and pour over the olive oil and vermouth. Turn the spears in the pan then sit them cut-side up again before putting into the oven to roast for 30 minutes until the leaves are slightly charred and wilted and the cores soft.

2   Take out of the oven and let the darkened, softened endive sit in the pan for 10 minutes before transferring to a plate, making sure you pour every bit of juice over. If there are any sticky caramelized bits in the pan, de-glaze with a spoonful of boiling water and pour over, too. Strew with thyme and serve.

BUTTERNUT AND SWEET POTATO CURRY

This is a rambunctiously vibrant curry, both to look at and eat. It is rich, sweet, and hearty, with tomatoes providing a balancing acidity and the curry paste bringing uncompromising fire. Of course chiles do vary in heat, so if you're after something a little less passage-clearing, use two rather than three, and if you want to go milder still, simply seed the chiles. Having said that, cooking with chiles always has a touch of roulette about it.

While I have indicated to add the creamy top bit of the coconut milk first, I have to say that I all too often, not paying attention, open the can upside down, so don't worry too much about it, but still add just a little of the coconut milk first, stirring it into the pan with the paste, before pouring in the rest.

I like the drama of black Venus rice or Black Forbidden Rice with this, but by all means serve any rice you want alongside.

For make ahead/store notes see p.275

1   Blitz the prepared onion, chiles, ginger, garlic, turmeric, ground coriander, cinnamon, and salt to a paste with an immersion blender.

2   Heat the coconut or vegetable oil in a wide heavy-based Dutch oven that has a lid, and then fry the paste for about a minute or so, stirring well. Don't use a wooden spoon unless you don't mind it being stained by the turmeric.

3   Open the can of coconut milk carefully and then scrape off the creamy top into the paste, stirring everything together over the heat for another minute or so before adding the rest of the can of coconut milk, followed by the broth, canned tomatoes, then the chunked sweet potato and butternut.

4   Give a good stir, bring to a boil, and, once bubbling, turn down the heat, and when everything is gently simmering, clamp on the lid and cook for 40–50 minutes (though start checking at 30) until the sweet potatoes are soft and the squash cooked through. Check for seasoning, then leave to stand off the heat for 10 minutes or so before serving.

5   Eat with the rice and put chopped cilantro and lime wedges on the table alongside, for sprinkling and spritzing respectively, or serve with the Cilantro and Jalapeño Salsa on p.104.

SERVES 4–6

Red onion – 1, peeled and cut into chunks
Red chiles – 2–3 (see recipe introduction), stalks removed and cut into 3
Fresh ginger – 3-inch piece, peeled and cut into thick coins
Garlic – 2 cloves, peeled and halved
Fresh turmeric – 3-inch piece, peeled and roughly chopped, or 1 teaspoon of ground turmeric
Ground coriander – 1 teaspoon
Ground cinnamon – ½ teaspoon
Sea salt flakes or kosher salt – 1 teaspoon, or to taste
Coconut oil or vegetable oil – 2 tablespoons
Coconut milk – 1 x 14-ounce can
Vegetable broth – 1½ cups
Canned diced tomatoes – 1 x 14-ounce can
Sweet potatoes – 1 pound (approx. 3), peeled and cut into large bite-sized pieces, to give 3 cups loosely packed
Butternut squash – 1 (2–2½ pounds), peeled, seeded, and cut into bite-sized pieces, to give 7 cups loosely packed

To serve:
Rice
Cilantro and limes
or
Cilantro and Jalapeño Salsa
(see p.104)

GARLIC AND PARMESAN MASHED POTATOES

I'm not, as a rule, one for flavoring mashed potatoes, but this version is a worthy exception. Because the garlic cloves are boiled with the potatoes, they make their presence felt sweetly rather than shoutily, and the Parmesan provides a gentle tang. Bizarre though this may sound, I actually have a dedicated electric potato mashing tool (in my defense, I was given it as a present) which makes the potatoes smooth and airy at the same time. You can easily approximate this by giving the potatoes a quick go with an electric hand whisk once you've roughly mashed them by hand. But in all cases, the Parmesan must be stirred in by hand at the end. Do not consider using a blender or processor, as both will turn your mash gluey.

It would be criminal of me not to mention that the water the potatoes are cooked in makes the best vegetable soup in the world. I generally make a pea soup with it, cooking 5½ cups of frozen petits pois in just over 4 cups of potato and garlic broth, until very soft, and then blitzing till smooth with an immersion blender. And you don't have to rush to use it; it's fine, so long as it's in the fridge, for up to five days.

While mashed potatoes are always best made at the last minute, you can turn this into an easy make-ahead mash, reformulating it as a gratin. It is worth noting that any leftovers make fabulous potato waffles, see p.71.

SERVES 6–8 WITH – IF YOU'RE LUCKY – LEFTOVERS TO MAKE THE WAFFLES ON P.71

Potatoes, such as Yukon Gold – 4½ pounds, peeled and cut into large equal-sized chunks
Garlic – 8 fat cloves, bruised and slightly splintered with the flat side of a wide-bladed knife, then slipped out of their skins
Sea salt flakes or kosher salt – 2 teaspoons, plus more to taste
Unsalted butter – 5 tablespoons, soft
Parmesan – ½ cup finely grated

For the optional topping:
Dried bread crumbs or panko – ½ cup
Unsalted butter – 3 tablespoons, soft, in blobs or teaspoons
Parmesan – ⅓ cup finely grated

For make ahead/store notes see p.275

1   Put the prepared potatoes and garlic into a very large saucepan, cover with cold water, add the salt, put on the lid, and bring to a boil over a high heat, then turn down and cook partially covered – just a crack – until very tender.

2   Put a colander over a large bowl or another saucepan and drain the potatoes, letting the starchy water collect underneath. Do not throw this away: it is precious liquid (see recipe introduction).

3   Add the butter to the hot, emptied-out potato pan, and let it start melting, then tip in the drained potatoes and garlic. Dip a measuring cup into the cooking liquid, add about ½ cup, and mash using your chosen method (see recipe introduction). You may want to add another ½ cupful or so of cooking liquid. I never add less than 1 cup, as I like this to be as smooth and creamy as possible, though I'm aware many people prefer more solid mashed potatoes. (Again: do not throw away any leftover liquid.) Stir the Parmesan in by hand and check for seasoning before transferring to a warm bowl.

4   If you are making this in advance, butter a small roasting pan or ovenproof dish, measuring approx. 9 × 13 inches, and fill with the mashed potatoes, smoothing down the top. Leave to cool, then refrigerate, covered, for up to 3 days. On reheating, remove from the fridge and let come to room temperature, which will take an hour or two, depending on the weather. Preheat the oven to 400°F and make a crumbly topping by rubbing the bread crumbs or panko together with the butter and Parmesan, then dot and sprinkle on top. Cook for about 30 minutes, or until piping hot all the way through. Loosely cover the dish with aluminum foil if the topping is getting too brown at any stage.

POTATO WAFFLES
FROM LEFTOVER GARLIC AND PARMESAN MASHED POTATOES

I GET 1 BATCH OUT OF MY
IRON, WHICH AMOUNTS TO
4 SMALL WAFFLES

**Leftover Garlic and Parmesan
Mashed Potatoes (see p.66)** – 1 cup
Unsalted butter – 2 tablespoons,
melted and cooled a little
Whole milk – ¼ cup, at room
temperature
Egg – 1 large, at room temperature
Parmesan – 1 tablespoon finely grated
Scallion – 1, thinly sliced
Cornstarch – 2 tablespoons
Baking powder – ½ teaspoon

To serve:
Crisp bacon

There is nothing to stop you making these with regular leftover mashed potatoes, in which case you would have to season boisterously, adding minced garlic and a little extra Parmesan before proceeding as below. Bear in mind this recipe is based on your having just one cupful of potatoes left, so scale up accordingly if you have more potatoes asking to be used up.

For make ahead/store notes see p.275

1   Put the leftover Garlic and Parmesan Mashed Potatoes into a bowl and beat it with a fork a little, just to loosen it.

2   Whisk the slightly cooled melted butter, milk, and egg together in a pitcher and then add to the mashed potatoes, gently beating it in as you go. Add the Parmesan, scallion, cornstarch, and baking powder, and continue to whisk or beat (I do all this with a small, flat hand whisk) until there are no lumps.

3   Prepare and heat the waffle iron following the manufacturer's instructions.

4   Fill your heated waffle iron with batter, spreading it out slightly with a heatproof spatula, if necessary, and close with the other heated half of the waffle iron. In my stove-top waffle iron, they need 3 minutes on the first side, then 4 on the second, once it's been turned over; if you're using a different contraption, follow the manual's timing instructions. Once cooked, the waffles should be golden brown and crisp on the outside.

5   Ease out the cooked waffle, separate it into four, and serve with the accompaniments of your choice. I fry bacon to eat with, dripping some of the bacon fat over the waffles before topping with the crisp slices. But they are also a sterling addition to a proper old-fashioned full English breakfast.

RED CABBAGE WITH CRANBERRIES

The sweetness of a long-braised red cabbage is perfectly punctuated by the cheek-squeaky sharpness of cranberries. And, if you let this stand a little before serving, they – most desirably – help to thicken the juices the cabbage gives off as it cooks. Indeed, I always make red cabbage ahead of time: think of it as a vegetable stew, which is better, as all stews are, when the flavors are left to mellow and merge with one another. If you are following suit, then you can cook the cabbage for slightly less than its full time, as it will continue to cook on reheating.

Even a small red cabbage seems to make enough to feed an army, but I can't see the point of leaving half a red cabbage lingering in the fridge. If you're feeding less than a crowd, just stash what you don't need in airtight containers in the deep freeze, ready to provide warm succor on cold winter nights.

For make ahead/store notes see p.275

For make ahead/store notes see p.275

SERVES 8–10

Red cabbage – 1 small head (approx. 2 pounds), sliced
Red onion – 1 large (approx. 7 ounces), peeled and sliced into thin half-moons
Dark brown sugar – 2 tablespoons
Ground cinnamon – 2 teaspoons
Ground cloves – ¼ teaspoon
Dried cranberries – 1 cup
Fresh or frozen cranberries – 2 cups
Sea salt flakes or kosher salt – 4 teaspoons
Apple juice – 3 cups

1   Put all the ingredients into a large, heavy-based saucepan that comes with a lid, and give a good stir.

2   Bring to a boil over a high heat, stir again, let it bubble away for 10 minutes, then clamp on the lid, lower the heat, and leave to simmer for 1½–2 hours, or until tender.

SMASHED CHICKPEAS
WITH GARLIC, LEMON, AND CHILE

There is not a way I don't like a chickpea or, indeed, a time when I couldn't eat mashed potatoes, and this is a very happy combination of both, while being very gratifyingly its own thing. It offers comfort, uplift, aromatic zing, and ease – just what you want when lacking time or energy or both. While I eat this all the year round, I do think of it as the perfect summer version of a bowl of wintry mashed potatoes. And cold, this bumpy chickpea mash is wonderful as a kind of tahini-free hummus.

I use jarred chickpeas mostly; canned chickpeas are often too pebbly, I find. Obviously you can use dried chickpeas that you've soaked and cooked to velvety softness, if you're prepared to wait. And whether you're using fat chickpeas out of a jar or ones you've cooked yourself, don't drain them too meticulously: a little of the gloopy liquid that clings to the chickpeas is a good thing here.

For make ahead/store notes see p.275

For make ahead/store notes see p.275

SERVES 4–6

Regular olive oil – 3 tablespoons
Garlic – 2 fat cloves, peeled and minced
Lemons – 2, finely grated zest of 1, plus ¼ cup of juice
Red chile – 1, seeded and very finely chopped
Chickpeas – 6 cups, drained (2 x 25-ounce jars or 4 x 16-ounce cans)
Sea salt flakes or kosher salt – to taste
Extra-virgin olive oil – a few glugs

1   Warm the regular olive oil in a heavy-based saucepan that comes with a lid then, over a low heat, stir in the garlic, followed by the lemon zest. After 30 seconds or so of pushing around the pan with a wooden spoon, or whatever you use, just to make sure the garlicky zest doesn't stick to the pan, add most of the chopped chile (saving some just to sprinkle over at the end) and stir for ½–1 minute, by which time the pan will be spicily fragrant, and the chile will become translucent orange, turning the lemony, garlicky oil a rich yellow. It's all very Tequila Sunrise.

2   Turn the heat up to medium, add the chickpeas along with 3 tablespoons of lemon juice, and stir gently so that they're slicked in the aromatic oil and flecked with chile, then cover, turn down the heat, and let cook gently for 5–10 minutes until warmed all the way through. Take the pan off the heat, remove the lid, and leave for a few minutes before smashing the chickpeas roughly with an old-school potato masher, just until you have a fuzzy rubble. Leave for a few minutes longer, so that they are warm – or even room temperature. If you want to leave them longer than 10 minutes, just put a lid on.

3   Just before serving add the remaining tablespoon of lemon juice as well as salt to taste, then drizzle with extra-virgin olive oil, scatter with the rest of the chile, and take to the table.

BRUSSELS SPROUTS WITH PRESERVED LEMONS AND POMEGRANATE

There is a vociferous anti-sprout brigade, but I have no time for their Brussels-bashing bigotry: I like sprouts in their traditional incarnation; as well as roasted till charred in a hot oven; thinly sliced and stir-fried; shredded and in a salad. This exotic casserole is my new favorite way of eating them.

For make ahead/store notes see p.275

1   Heat the oil and butter in a Dutch oven or heavy-based saucepan that has a lid, and fry the sliced leek, stirring occasionally, for about 5 minutes over a medium-high heat until softened but not browned.

2   Add the minced garlic and finely chopped preserved lemon and stir again, before adding the ground cinnamon.

3   Now add the halved sprouts and turn them in the pan to get them really well coated before sprinkling with the salt and pouring the water into the pan.

4   Stir again, then clamp on the lid and cook them over a medium-high heat for 3–5 minutes until they are tender, but not soft.

5   Once they are ready, stir through about three quarters of the chopped parsley and 2 tablespoons of the pomegranate seeds, and turn out into a bowl. Sprinkle with the remaining parsley and pomegranate seeds, and serve.

SERVES 4–6

Regular olive oil – 2 tablespoons
Unsalted butter – 2 tablespoons
Leek – 1, trimmed and thinly sliced
Garlic – 2 cloves, peeled and minced
Preserved lemons – 2 small, finely chopped, to give 3 tablespoons
Ground cinnamon – 1 teaspoon
Brussels sprouts – 1¾ pounds, trimmed and halved from root to tip
Sea salt flakes or kosher salt – 2 teaspoons
Water from a freshly boiled kettle – ½ cup
Italian parsley – leaves from a small bunch, roughly chopped, to give ⅓ cup loosely packed
Pomegranate seeds – ¼ cup

GARLICKY ROASTED POTATOES
WITH OREGANO AND FETA

SERVES 4–6

Potatoes – 2¾ pounds, unpeeled and cut into 1-inch cubes
Regular olive oil – ¼ cup
Garlic – 6 fat cloves, peeled and minced
Dried oregano – 2½ teaspoons
Feta cheese – 4 ounces, crumbled, to give 1 cup loosely packed

To serve:
Fresh oregano

When I was last in Melbourne, I ate some of the best fries of my life at one of George Calombaris's restaurants, Gazi: fried in punchy, garlic-steeped oil, golden and crunchy on the outside, fluffy within and, just out of the pan, tossed with dried oregano and crumbled feta. Generally a rather prissy fry purist, I was won over to the point of obsession – beyond the point of obsession – by these.

I haven't tried to emulate them but, instead, present my simple homespun version: no deep-fat frying involved; deep happiness achieved.

It is not advisable to make ahead/store

1   Preheat the oven to 425°F and tumble the potatoes into a shallow roasting pan or pans, large enough for the potatoes to sit in one layer. Toss in the oil, followed by the garlic and dried oregano, and roast in the oven for 50–60 minutes until crisp and golden, and cooked through.

2   Transfer to a serving bowl and toss with most of the feta, then sprinkle the remaining feta crumbles on top. If you have any fresh oregano on hand, strew away.

MOROCCAN VEGETABLE POT

This warmly-spiced vegetable stew, sweet with parsnips and carrots and tangy with preserved lemons and dried apricots, has become a regular in my house. While I generally eat it as a main course with the couscous that follows on p.83, it is a great accompaniment to a roast chicken, which would make it go a lot further, too. Either way, I always hope for leftovers: like all stews, this is wonderful eaten when it has had a day or two in the fridge; just bear in mind you'll need to add more water when you reheat it.

For make ahead/store notes see p.275

1   Warm the oil in a large-ish, heavy-based Dutch oven that has a tight-fitting lid and add the sliced leek, cumin seeds, ground ginger, and cinnamon stick (or sticks) and cook, stirring, for a minute or so.

2   Add the chopped carrots, parsnips, eggplant, and potatoes along with the garlic, chickpeas, olives, apricots, and preserved lemons. Pour in the water, sprinkle in the saffron and salt, give the pot a good stir, and let it all come to a boil, before putting on the lid, turning the heat down, and simmering for 35–45 minutes, or until the vegetables are tender, adding a little more water should the liquid have evaporated too much.

3   Let your pot stand off the heat for 10–15 minutes before serving, sprinkled with chopped cilantro. During which time you could be making the couscous on p.83.

SERVES 4–6

Regular olive oil – 1 tablespoon
Leek – 1 medium, trimmed and cut into approx. ¼-inch slices
Cumin seeds – 1 teaspoon
Ground ginger – 1 teaspoon
Cinnamon sticks – 1 long, or 2 short
Carrots – 2 medium-large, peeled and cut into chunky batons
Parsnips – 2 medium-large, peeled and cut into large bite-sized chunks
Eggplant – 1 medium-large, cut into large bite-sized chunks
Potato – 1 large, peeled and cut into bite-sized chunks
Garlic – 4 cloves, bruised and slightly splintered with the flat side of a wide-bladed knife, then slipped out of their skins
Chickpeas – 3 cups, drained (1 x 25-ounce jar or 2 x 16-ounce cans)
Small pitted green olives – ½ cup
Soft dried apricots – ⅔ cup, halved
Preserved lemons – 3 small, finely chopped, to give heaping ¼ cup
Cold water – 4 cups, or more as needed
Saffron threads – a fat pinch
Sea salt flakes or kosher salt – 2 teaspoons

To serve:
Cilantro

COUSCOUS WITH PINE NUTS AND DILL

Whole wheat couscous – 2 cups
**Vegetable bouillon powder or
concentrate** – 1½ teaspoons
Dried dill – 1½ teaspoons
**Water from a freshly boiled
kettle** – 2⅓ cups
Regular olive oil – 1 teaspoon
Pine nuts – ½ cup, toasted
Fresh dill – 2 tablespoons roughly
chopped, plus a few intact fronds
Sea salt flakes or kosher salt –
to taste

I have recently discovered whole wheat couscous, and now there is no turning back. It's slightly nuttier than regular couscous, though with none of the heavy chewiness of brown rice.

Any leftovers can be reheated, or eaten cold as a salad with other good things you may have in your fridge stirred into it, along with your finest olive oil and lemon juice.

For make ahead/store notes see p.275

1   Put the couscous into a fairly wide and shallow saucepan or dish, add the bouillon powder, or concentrate, and dried dill and then the freshly boiled water and the oil, giving everything a good stir. Immediately clamp on a tight-fitting lid or cover with a plate and leave for 15 minutes.

2   Uncover, and use a fork to break up the couscous until fluffed up into free-flowing grains, and then fork through about three-quarters of the toasted pine nuts and 1 tablespoon of fresh dill.

3   Check to see if you want to add any salt, then turn into a warmed serving dish and sprinkle with the remaining pine nuts and dill.

SWEET POTATO TACOS
WITH AVOCADO AND CILANTRO SAUCE AND A TOMATO AND PEAR RELISH

Given the choice between a crisp, curled-up taco-boat and the softshell wrap approach, I go for the latter every time. I don't wish to be too dictatorial about how you eat these tacos, but my advice is this: line a warm corn tortilla with shredded lettuce, top with both sweet potato and dill pickle wedges, dollop on avocado sauce then spoon some tomato and pear relish over the top. Fold together as best you can and don't eat in front of anyone you're not comfortable with. And by the way, the sweet potato wedges, just as they are, make a generous serving for two. I love them dipped into Golden Garlic Mayonnaise on p.115, too.

For make ahead/store notes see p.275

1 Preheat the oven to 400°F. Tumble the wedges onto a large, non-stick baking sheet. Mix the spices and baking powder together, then shake over the sweet potatoes and, taking a couple of spatulas, turn them patiently until lightly coated with the spices. Pour the oil over and toss and turn again, arranging the wedges in a single layer. Sprinkle with salt and roast in the oven for 35–40 minutes until cooked through and richly browned in parts.

2 You can get on with the relish and sauce once the sweet potatoes are in the oven. Mix the diced tomatoes, pear, and jalapeño together in a bowl. Add 2 teaspoons of lime juice and the salt, then toss together and taste to see whether you need any more lime juice or, indeed, salt.

3 To make the sauce, halve the avocado, remove the pit, and spoon the flesh into a bowl. Add the yogurt, cumin, salt, lime juice, and cilantro, then blitz with an immersion blender until smooth and flecked with green. Check for seasoning before serving.

4 Once the sweet potatoes are cooked, take them out of the oven and turn off the oven. Make a baggy – but tightly sealed – aluminum foil parcel for the tortillas, and leave to warm up in the residual heat of the oven.

5 Arrange everything else on the table, then bring the heated tortillas and get cracking.

SERVES 3–4

For the sweet potato wedges:
Sweet potatoes – 1¼ pounds (approx. 3–4), cut into skinny wedges
Ground cumin – 1 teaspoon
Paprika – 1 teaspoon
Baking powder – ½ teaspoon
Regular olive oil – 2 tablespoons
Sea salt flakes or kosher salt – 1 teaspoon

For the tomato and pear relish:
Tomatoes – 2 regular-sized, seeded and cut into very small dice, to give ⅔ cup loosely packed
Unripe pear – 1 small, peeled, cored, and cut into very small dice, to give ¾ cup loosely packed
Fresh jalapeño chile – 1, seeded and cut into very small dice
Lime – 2–3 teaspoons of juice
Sea salt flakes or kosher salt – ½ teaspoon

For the avocado sauce:
Soft ripe avocado – 1 fairly small
Plain whole milk yogurt – ½ cup, though use coconut-milk yogurt if this is to be vegan-pleasing
Ground cumin – 1 teaspoon
Sea salt flakes or kosher salt – ½ teaspoon
Lime – 2 teaspoons of juice
Cilantro – small bunch, stalks and all

To serve:
Corn tortillas – 6–8
Iceberg lettuce – shredded
Dill pickles – cut into wedges

TOMATO AND HORSERADISH SALAD

SERVES 4–6

Horseradish root – ¼ cup finely grated
Raw unfiltered apple cider vinegar – 2 tablespoons
Regular olive oil – 3 tablespoons
Sea salt flakes or kosher salt – 1 teaspoon
Sugar – a pinch
Cherry or grape tomatoes – 1¼ pounds (3½–4 cups), halved across the equator
Italian parsley – leaves from a small bunch, very roughly chopped, to give 1 cup loosely packed

One of the most gratifying things for a home cook is to scrummage a meal together out of leftovers. It's enormously satisfying to ransack the fridge and use up what lies under plastic wrap or is lounging about in the vegetable drawer; it always provides a relaxed, unforced creativity. I certainly would never have thought of using horseradish as a dressing for a tomato salad if I hadn't wanted to find a way to use up a horseradish root staring beseechingly at me every time I opened the fridge.

While obviously excellent with beef, and do consider the Flat Iron Steak and Roast Top Round on p.190 and p.194 respectively, this is wonderful with any oily fish, too.

To eat this at its best, leave time for the tomatoes to steep in the piquant dressing before serving.

For make ahead/store notes see p.275

1   Stir the grated horseradish and vinegar together in a small bowl, then add the oil, salt, and sugar and whisk a little with a fork, just to combine. Cover with plastic wrap and let stand for a while, if time permits.

2   Tumble the halved tomatoes into a large mixing bowl, add the dressing, and mix everything gently but thoroughly together. Cover the bowl with plastic wrap and leave for 30–60 minutes, by which time the tomatoes will have given out their fruity juices, which duly mingle with the fierceness of the horseradish.

3   Toss the tomatoes tenderly in their bowl, then add the parsley leaves and toss again gently. Decant to a smaller serving bowl or a large plate and take to the table.

QUINOA SALAD
WITH WALNUTS, RADISHES, AND POMEGRANATE

I'm slightly embarrassed to admit this (as well I might be), but since quinoa has become such a byword for clichéd trendy eating fads, I have been somewhat reluctant to print recipes for it. And yet, I eat it often, and gladly. This salad is no stranger to my table; not only is it incredibly easy to make (ideal when you're catering for big numbers), but leftovers produce excellent packed lunches for later in the week. And its herby lightness and fresh crunch are sublime.

For make ahead/store notes see p.275

1   If you have a rice cooker, I advise you to use it to cook the quinoa; it's the easiest way to go. Otherwise, put the quinoa into a heavy-based saucepan that comes with a tight-fitting lid, and pour the water over it. Bring it back to a boil over a high heat, then turn down and let simmer gently without the lid for 15 minutes, by which time all the water should be absorbed. Turn off the heat, cover the pan with a clean tea towel, clamp on the lid, and leave for a further 15 minutes to dry out, though you can leave it like this for up to 40 minutes, if wished. Fluff with a fork and turn out into a wide shallow dish. Add the salt, lemon zest (reserving the juice for later), and olive oil, then fork to mix through, and leave to cool.

2   When the quinoa is cold, add the radishes, followed by the walnut pieces (breaking them up a little in your fingers as you do so), the mint and lemon juice and most of the pomegranate seeds, cilantro, and parsley.

3   Toss lightly to mix, making sure everything is well combined, then taste to see if you want more salt before turning out into a bowl. Sprinkle with the remaining pomegranate seeds, cilantro, and parsley on serving.

SERVES 6–8

White quinoa – 1⅔ cups
Water from a freshly boiled kettle – 3 cups
Sea salt flakes or kosher salt – 1 teaspoon, or to taste
Lemon – 1, finely grated zest and juice
Extra-virgin olive oil – ¼ cup
Radishes – 7 ounces, quartered, to give 1⅔ cups loosely packed
Walnut pieces – 1 cup
Mint – 2 tablespoons finely chopped leaves
Pomegranate seeds – ¾ cup
Cilantro – leaves from a medium bunch, finely chopped, to give 2 cups loosely packed
Italian parsley – leaves from a medium bunch, finely chopped, to give 2 cups loosely packed

RADICCHIO, CHESTNUT, AND BLUE CHEESE SALAD
WITH A CITRUS, WHOLE GRAIN MUSTARD, AND HONEY DRESSING

SERVES 4–6

For the dressing:

Lime – 2 teaspoons of juice

Orange – 2 teaspoons of juice

Whole grain mustard – 1 teaspoon

Honey – 1 teaspoon

Regular olive oil – 1 tablespoon

Asian sesame oil – a drop

Sea salt flakes or kosher salt –
a fat pinch

For the salad:

Radicchio – 1 large or 2 small
(12–14 ounces total weight), torn into
bite-sized pieces

**Ready-cooked chestnuts from a
package, jar, or can** – ¾ cup, broken
up into small pieces

Sharp (not creamy) blue cheese –
4 ounces, fridge-cold, crumbled, to give
1 cup loosely packed

Bitter leaves, salty cheese, sweet waxy chestnuts: this is a winter salad that I can't confine myself to eating just in season. I generally go for Gorgonzola or Stilton here, but essentially what you need is blue cheese that will crumble well without going into buttery clumps. And while I would never normally condone putting either in the fridge, here the cheese must be cold so that you can crumble it.

I make this dressing – which truly deserves stand-alone billing – a lot. It's perfect with all robust bitter leaves, but, used a little more sparingly, also with any lettuce with a bit of crunch to it. When I want more than just a sprinkle of salt, a spritz of lemon juice, and a glug of extra-virgin olive oil on a salad, this has now become my default dressing, and I make it in weekly batches.

And I can report that you can use walnuts rather than chestnuts very successfully here, too.

For make ahead/store notes see p.275

1   Put all the dressing ingredients in a small glass jar and shake to mix, or whisk together in a small pitcher or bowl.

2   Put the torn-up pieces of radicchio into a large mixing bowl. Pour the dressing over them and toss patiently and well. Add the broken-up chestnuts and most of the crumbled blue cheese and toss again, gently but thoroughly, then tip into a serving bowl and sprinkle the remaining blue cheese on top.

CHOPPED SALAD

This is very far from the American classic, but – at least in its starting point – rather more Lebanese in style. I've added pomegranate seeds to the herb-flecked dice, not as a picturesque garnish, though it's certainly true that even a garnish (and, oh, how I loathe that word) must add more than beauty, but because I feel them to be an essential ingredient here, giving crunch and tangy sweetness.

I often eat this alongside the Lamb Kofta on p.168 but it graces any table it is brought to.

For make ahead/store notes see p.275

1   Put everything except for the parsley into a large mixing bowl and toss together very well. Let stand for 10 minutes.

2   Add the parsley, toss again until everything is a beautiful jumble, and serve immediately.

SERVES 4–6

Zucchini – 1 small, peeled in stripes and cut into small dice, to give scant 1 cup loosely packed

English cucumber – ½, peeled in stripes, seeded and cut into small dice, to give 1 cup loosely packed

Scallions – 4, white and pale green part only, thinly sliced

Tomatoes – 4 regular-sized, seeded and cut into small dice, to give scant 1¼ cups loosely packed

Garlic – 1 clove, peeled and minced

Pomegranate seeds – 1 cup

Dried mint – 1 teaspoon

Dried dill – 1 teaspoon

Sea salt flakes or kosher salt – 1 teaspoon, plus more to taste

Lemon – 1, finely grated zest and juice

Extra-virgin olive oil – 2 tablespoons

Italian parsley – leaves from a large bunch, roughly chopped, to give 4 cups loosely packed

BEET AND GOAT CHEESE SALAD
WITH A PASSIONFRUIT DRESSING

The trauma of school cafeteria food can leave its mark, and it took many years until I was able to approach beets with anything other than dread. My rehabilitation started with eating them raw, coarsely grated in a salad, but once I'd discovered how good they were wrapped in aluminum foil and roasted in a hot oven, my conversion was complete.

It's perhaps immodest to say it, but I am enormously proud of the passionfruit dressing. I'm not sure anyone would guess what it is providing the scented acidity – no one has so far – but its incomparable fruity sharpness is the perfect foil to this rich, ruby root vegetable, its sweetness in turn beautifully balanced by the saltiness of the goat cheese.

For make ahead/store notes see p.276

SERVES 3–4

Beets – 1 pound
Passionfruit – 2
Sea salt flakes or kosher salt – a fat pinch
Extra-virgin olive oil – 1 tablespoon
Goat cheese – 4 ounces, crumbled, to give 1 cup loosely packed
Dill – a few fronds

1   Preheat the oven to 425°F. Wrap each beet individually in aluminum foil, making a baggy but tightly sealed parcel. Sit these on a baking sheet. Otherwise line a baking dish or roasting pan with foil, put in the beets, and make a tightly sealed roof with another piece of foil; or use a disposable foil pan and cover similarly.

2   Bake in the oven until they are cooked, and the tip of a knife goes through easily. I find that large beets take 2 or even 3 hours, smaller ones can take half this time, though it's worth checking earlier; just make sure you seal everything up tightly again if more cooking time is required. When they're ready, leave them to cool, unwrapped, before removing their skins. You can help the process by giving them a gentle nudge with a sharp knife first, though you don't want to cut into the flesh. But what you do want – or I do – is to be wearing disposable vinyl gloves for this. Transfer the beets to a board, though not a wooden one, and cut into thin slices.

3   Put a strainer (you don't need a very large one for this) over a small bowl and cut a passionfruit in half, not going quite the whole way through (this is just to stop any of their precious juices spilling out onto the cutting board). Hold the passionfruit over the strainer and open it up, spooning out the pulp. Using a teaspoon, stir the pulp energetically, pushing down onto the strainer, so that the juice drips out and collects in the bowl. Now do the same with the other passionfruit; you should get about 4 teaspoons of juice in all. I can't really think of a good use for the discarded seeds, but give me time.

4   Add the salt to the passionfruit juice, followed by the oil, and stir
vigorously to blend.

5   Arrange the beets on a platter and crumble on the goat cheese,
then, giving the dressing a good stir again, pour it over and scatter
some feathery fronds of dill on top.

BASHED CUCUMBER AND RADISH SALAD

This is a distant relative of a Chinese cucumber salad, in which unpeeled cucumbers are seeded and chopped into relatively large pieces, bashed about a bit, then salted to remove excess liquid, before being tossed into an often fairly spiky dressing. I like to remove only half the skin from the cucumbers, but don't salt them – maybe I should, but I don't – and the dressing I toss them in (absorbed all the better by the cucumber for having been set upon with a meat tenderizer or other heavy weight) is fragrant rather than fierce. Plus, I add radishes, which is where I part company completely with the original inspiration. For me, they are the perfect partner here: they bring their own cheery-cheeked crunch, distinct pepperiness, and rosy beauty. But if you wish to create a salad of calm, jade purity, then you may do without them and simply add more cucumber.

It is not advisable to make ahead/store

1   In a large bowl mix the vinegar, salt, sugar, garlic, and ginger.

2   Peel the cucumbers in stripes – that's to say, use a vegetable peeler to shave the skin off in strips so that you have dark-and-pale-green-striped cucumbers – then halve them lengthways and, with the tip of a teaspoon, scoop out the seeds. Chop the seeded cucumbers into approx. 1½ inch long chunks.

3   With the pieces cut-side up on a cutting board, bash them with, for choice, the spiky side of a meat tenderizer, but a can of tomatoes does the job well, too. Most of the pieces of cucumber will split as you bash them. But don't go ballistic here, or you'll have the cucumber skeetering off the board in all directions. A firm, not frenzied, hand is all that's required.

4   Add the cucumber pieces to the dressing, turn them well in it, and leave for 15–20 minutes.

5   Finally, add the radish halves, sesame oil, and sesame seeds, toss to mix and serve immediately.

SERVES 4–6

Rice wine vinegar – 3 tablespoons
Sea salt flakes or kosher salt – 1 teaspoon
Sugar – 2 teaspoons
Garlic – 1 fat clove, peeled and minced
Fresh ginger – 1 teaspoon finely grated
English cucumbers – 2 medium, fridge-cold (approx. 1½ pounds total weight)
Radishes – 12 ounces, halved, to give scant 3 cups
Asian sesame oil – 1 teaspoon
Black sesame seeds – 1 teaspoon

SUBVERTING THE SPIRALIZER

If you are one of the fad-resistant few who have either never bought a spiralizer or don't even know what one is, turn the page now. Don't give it another thought. But, mindful of the several tons of spiralizers lying dormant in kitchen cupboards up and down the length of the country, I have found a new use for them.

While you will never find me making zoodles or allowing any other vegetable to masquerade as pasta, I can say this for my spiralizer: it does make very fine shoestring fries.

For make ahead/store notes see p.276

For make ahead/store notes see p.276

SERVES 3–4

Potatoes, such as Yukon Gold – preferably large, 1 pound, peeled
Vegetable oil – approx. 4 cups or as needed
Sea salt flakes or kosher salt – to taste

1   Spiralize your peeled potatoes using the fine round cutter – all machines come with their own instructions – so that you have skinny coils of potato. Divide them into three equal piles on a clean tea towel and wrap them in it to absorb excess moisture.

2   Get out a baking sheet and a large plate and line both with a double layer of paper towels. Set both by the stove. Preheat the oven to 250°F.

3   Pour the oil into a wide saucepan – I use one of 9 inch diameter, and don't advise you go any smaller – to come up about 1¼ inches deep and heat the oil until a cube of bread sizzles when dropped into it.

4   When the oil is hot enough, carefully drop in the first batch of potato coils and fry for 5–6 minutes, stirring them gently with tongs or a mesh ladle from time to time, to make sure they aren't sticking to the bottom. Once golden brown, carefully lift using a mesh ladle or slotted spoon and place on the lined baking sheet. Put the sheet in the oven.

5   Proceed with the second batch. When ready, transfer with your mesh ladle to the paper-lined plate and, taking the oil off the heat momentarily, add this second batch to the shoestring fries keeping warm in the oven.

6   Put the oil back on the heat, and fry the last batch.

7   Tip all onto a large plate, sprinkle generously with salt, and eat immediately. But you don't need me to tell you that, do you?

SPICED ALMONDS

SERVES 4

Ground cumin – ½ teaspoon
Ground coriander – ½ teaspoon
Ground cinnamon – ½ teaspoon
Cayenne pepper – ½ teaspoon
Vegetable oil – 1 tablespoon
Honey – 1 teaspoon
Lime – 1, finely grated zest
Sea salt flakes or kosher salt –
1 teaspoon, plus more to taste
Skinned almonds – 2 cups

I'm not lying to you when I say that there are enough nuts here for four people to pick on very happily over cocktails. But however many you make, you'll never have any left over. Two people could easily make short work of these. There's just something irresistible about this combination of crunch and kick.

The honey adds very little in the way of sweetness: rather it binds the heat of the spices and the sourness of the lime to the toasty almonds.

For make ahead/store notes see p.276

1   Preheat the oven to 350°F.

2   In a large bowl mix together – I find a silicone spatula best here – the cumin, coriander, cinnamon, cayenne, oil, honey, lime zest, and salt, until you have a scant, thick, rust-colored paste.

3   Scatter the almonds onto a baking sheet and cook in the oven for about 15 minutes (though check at 10), by which time the nuts should be colored slightly.

4   Quickly tip the hot, toasted almonds into the bowl you have ready and waiting with its paste, and stir briskly with your spatula until the nuts are lightly and evenly coated with the sticky spice mixture, with none left sticking to the bowl. This could take a couple of minutes. Add salt to taste, then transfer to a large plate to cool a little – this dries out and sets the spicy coating, and hardens the nuts – before decanting into a serving bowl or bowls. Know, too, that they're every bit as good completely cold, which means you can comfortably make them in advance.

CILANTRO AND JALAPEÑO SALSA

I have been making my version of a sauce I found on the Epicurious website for some time, and very indebted I am for the inspiration, for all that my take on it is heavier on the cilantro and lighter on the garlic and lime. Known simply as Green Sauce, this is a constant in my house: I just wouldn't be allowed not to have it in the fridge at all times. It can be eaten either as a condiment – and once you get the taste for it, you'll find yourself dolloping it alongside pretty much everything you eat – or a dip, specifically good with blue corn or unsalted tortilla chips. And don't be lulled by the cool greenness: this is – desirably – fierce and fiery. Even though I wouldn't – it's the unrelenting heat I love – you could, of course, seed the jalapeños. And although I haven't tried this with other green chiles, there is no reason why you couldn't.

For make ahead/store notes see p.276

MAKES APPROX. 1⅔ cups

Cilantro – large bunch, tender stalks and all, to give 4 cups roughly chopped
Fresh jalapeño chiles – 4–5, to give 1 cup roughly chopped
Garlic – 3 cloves, peeled and halved
Vegetable oil – ½ cup
Limes – 2, finely grated zest and ¼ cup of juice
Sea salt flakes or kosher salt – 1–2 teaspoons

1 With an immersion blender blitz the cilantro, jalapeños, garlic, oil, zest and juice of the limes, and 1 teaspoon of salt until you have a smooth and creamy, flecked sauce. Taste to see if you want to add any more salt.

2 If not eating immediately, transfer to a Mason jar or similar and refrigerate, though make sure you take it out in time to get to room temperature, and give the jar a good shake before serving.

RED-HOT ROASTED SALSA

Tomatoes – 1¾ pounds (approx.
8 large-ish), halved across the equator
Red chiles – 2 ounces (4–5)
Red onion – 1 large (approx. 7 ounces),
peeled and cut into eighths
Red bell peppers – 2, seeded and
each one cut into about 8 strips
Garlic – 4 fat cloves, peeled
Sea salt flakes or kosher salt –
1 teaspoon, plus more to taste
Vegetable oil – 2 tablespoons

Chiles, even of the same type, really do differ a lot in strength, so it can be difficult to calibrate the heat exactly but, with the number of chiles I use, this is either really fiery or really, really fiery. You can reduce the amount of chiles of course, but I like this to blow my head off.

While I first made this as a dip for tortilla chips, I must also recommend dolloping it alongside fried halloumi. Indeed, it makes – for fire-eaters – a wonderful all-round condiment, an incendiary ketchup to be splodged on whenever you're seeking flame and flavor.

For make ahead/store notes see p.276

1   Preheat the oven to 425°F. Put the halved tomatoes cut-side up in a roasting pan.

2   Arrange the whole red chiles around them, along with the red onion wedges, strips of red bell pepper, and the peeled garlic cloves.

3   Sprinkle with the salt, drizzle over the oil, and roast in the oven for about 40 minutes, or until everything is softened, with some charred edges.

4   Take out of the oven and leave for about 5 minutes, then carefully pull the stalks off the red chiles; they should come away easily.

5   Transfer everything, including any juices, into a bowl and blitz with an immersion blender, pulsing rather than blending continuously, so you can get the texture you want; I go for smoothish. Add salt to taste, and leave to cool before serving.

WHITE MISO HUMMUS

MAKES APPROX. 2 CUPS

Chickpeas – 3 cups drained
(1 x 25-ounce jar or 2 x 16-ounce
cans)
Garlic – 1 clove, peeled and halved
White miso – 3 tablespoons
Cold water – ¼ cup
Sea salt flakes or kosher salt –
½ teaspoon, or more to taste
Tahini – 2 tablespoons, at room
temperature
Lemon – 2 tablespoons of juice,
plus more to taste

To serve:
Asian sesame oil
Sesame seeds

While I freely concede that adding white miso to hummus produces something of a culinary culture clash, the result itself yields a deeply seductive spread. I must also confess that I have to stop myself adding white miso to pretty much anything I'm cooking: it always provides such depth and rich, smoky savoriness.

While it can be eaten as a dip, I like this best slathered on toast with a few more drops of Asian sesame oil and sprinkled with some sesame seeds; and for parties, you can spread it likewise on small, plain crackers.

As ever, I so much prefer to use the (usually Spanish) chickpeas that come in a jar, or dried ones I've cooked myself, but if push comes to shove you could use two cans of chickpeas.

You'll find it easier to measure out your tahini if it's at room temperature first, and give it a good stir before spooning out.

For make ahead/store notes see p.276

1   Put the drained chickpeas into a food processor along with the garlic, miso, and cold water and blitz till thoroughly combined.

2   Add the salt, tahini, and 2 tablespoons of lemon juice, and keep running the motor until smooth.

3   Taste for seasoning, adding more salt or lemon juice as needed, then decant into a serving bowl, and leave for about 30 minutes at room temperature for the flavor of the hummus to develop. Drizzle with sesame oil and sprinkle with sesame seeds on serving, if wished.

PEAR AND PASSIONFRUIT CHUTNEY

I love homemade preserves, but it is a stressful business. Making chutney is anything but. You just throw everything together in a saucepan and let it bubble away: no checking for setting points or running around the kitchen ransacking drawers trying to find the candy thermometer bought once in a flurry of domestic hopefulness.

This chutney, with the soft, sweet graininess of pears and the perfumed sharpness and crunch of passionfruit, is a particular joy. The only drawback is that you do need to leave it unopened, mellowing in its jar, for about a month before eating it. You'd be wise to make a new batch the minute you've cracked open the first.

You need sterilized jars to put the chutney in, but I consider a jar straight from the dishwasher (as long as the inside has not been touched) to be sterilized. Or wash the jars and lids in warm soapy water before rinsing and letting them dry in a cool (275°F) oven for 10 minutes.

For make ahead/store notes see p.276

For make ahead/store notes see p.276

MAKES APPROX. 2 CUPS

Pears (not too ripe) – 1¾ pounds (approx. 3 large), peeled, cored, and roughly chopped, to give 5 cups loosely packed

Onion – 1 large, peeled and roughly chopped, to give 1½ cups loosely packed

Passionfruit – 4, pulp and seeds

Turbinado sugar – ¾ cup plus 2 tablespoons

Sea salt flakes or kosher salt – 1 teaspoon

Pepper – a good grinding

Ground ginger – 2 teaspoons

Fresh ginger – 1 tablespoon finely grated

Ground turmeric – 1 teaspoon

Cider or white wine vinegar – 1½ cups

1 Put all the ingredients into a saucepan and give a stir before bringing everything to a boil, then reduce the heat slightly and cook at a brisk simmer, stirring every now and again, for 35–45 minutes until the mixture thickens.

2 Let the pan cool a little, and then spoon the chutney into a warm, sterilized jar or jars (see recipe introduction) then put the lids on and leave to cool.

GOLDEN GARLIC MAYONNAISE

MAKES APPROX. 1 CUP

Egg – 1 large, at room temperature
Saffron threads – ¼ teaspoon
Garlic – 2 cloves, peeled and halved
Lemon – 1 tablespoon of juice, plus
1 teaspoon
Sea salt flakes or kosher salt –
½ teaspoon
Cold water – 1 tablespoon
Regular olive oil – 1 cup

My mother was a firm believer in child labor, and much of my childhood was spent making mayonnaise the old-fashioned way. I'd stand at the blue formica kitchen table, with my bowl of egg yolks, whisking anxiously, as my sister, Thomasina, stood above me on a rickety chair, and slowly drip-dripped in the oil. And so I feel a frisson of nervous rebellion with this recipe, one which my mother would never have countenanced in her kitchen.

I know there are many short-cut mayonnaise recipes, but this one produces the perfect, old-school texture and yet is practically instant: the one-minute mayo. The method comes from the great J. Kenji López-Alt (known in my home simply as Mr. Serious Eats) and I've made a number of versions using it, but this – bright with saffron and brazen with garlic – is my favorite. I have gone quite condimental for it.

For make ahead/store notes see p.276

1   Put all the ingredients, except for the extra teaspoon of lemon juice, into the goblet that comes with your immersion blender. You can use a small bowl but it really needs to be a very snug fit around the head of your blender: it's what will make the mayo work.

2   Plant the immersion blender against the bottom of the goblet and then switch it on at full power, but don't move it around just yet. Again, this is important for the mayonnaise to come together.

3   Once the mayo starts to form around the head of the immersion blender, foaming up a little – and this shouldn't take more than about 30 seconds – you can move the head of the blender and keep whizzing to absorb the rest of the oil, creating a smooth, thick mayonnaise.

4   Transfer to a bowl, and stir in the teaspoonful of lemon juice by hand, which will loosen the texture a little. Cover with plastic wrap and leave to stand for at least 15 minutes. If you can bear to leave it for longer, so much the better: both flavor and golden hue will deepen further on standing; its true color emerges after it has been in the fridge overnight. Stir gently before serving, dispersing the flecks of saffron.

FLASH-FRIED SQUID
WITH TOMATO AND TEQUILA SALSA

A friend of mine recently asked me for a recipe that would go with a burger for the Berlin Bruisers' Bash-About, a gay and inclusive rugby club tournament. This salsa is what I came up with and it is now a favorite at my table.

Diamond-etching the squid makes it curl up jauntily and keeps it lusciously tender. And although I was initially hesitant about trying my hand at it, I can happily report that it is much more complicated to explain than it is to do.

For make ahead/store notes see p.276

SERVES 4

For the salsa:

Red onion – ½ small, peeled and cut into small dice, to give ¼ cup loosely packed

Tequila – 1 tablespoon

Lime – 2 tablespoons of juice

Tomatoes – 3 regular-sized, seeded and cut into small dice, to give 1 heaping cup loosely packed

Fresh jalapeño chile – 1, seeded and finely diced

Red chile – 1, seeded and finely diced

Sea salt flakes or kosher salt – 1 teaspoon

For the squid:

Medium squid – whole, cleaned, tubes and tentacles (approx. 1½ pounds cleaned weight)

Regular olive oil – 3 tablespoons

Sea salt flakes or kosher salt – ½ teaspoon

Pepper – a good grinding

Garlic – 2 cloves, peeled and minced

To serve:

Arugula leaves

1   Tip the prepared onion into a bowl and pour the tequila and lime juice over it. Stir well and tamp down a little. Leave it to steep for at least 15 minutes.

2   Stir in the tomatoes, jalapeño, red chile, and salt and taste a little to see if any more salt is needed. Set aside while you get on with the squid.

3   Put the tentacles into a bowl big enough to take all the rest of the squid later.

4   Slice open one of the squid tubes and lay it out flat on a cutting board, with the inside facing up and the narrow end at the top. Using a sharp knife, score deep diagonal lines into the flesh, but be careful not to cut all the way through. Score lines in the other direction to make a diamond pattern.

5   Cut the scored squid tube into approximately 2-inch squares and put the pieces in the bowl with the tentacles. Repeat with the remaining tubes. Add the oil, salt, pepper, and garlic to the bowl of prepared squid, and give it a good stir to ensure it's all evenly coated.

6   Heat a large, heavy-based frying pan until very hot. You don't need to add oil to the pan, as you've added the oil to the squid. Working in batches, drop the scored squid tubes into the pan – it doesn't matter which way up they land – and let them cook over a high heat, turning them regularly with tongs, for about 2 minutes, or until they have lost their translucency and are just cooked through. The pieces will curl up with a very visible diamond pattern.

7   Transfer to a large plate or bowl as you go. Once all these pieces are cooked, add the tentacles to the pan and fry, stirring regularly, until curly and cooked through.

8   Arrange on some arugula leaves and serve with the tomato and tequila salsa on the side, sprinkling some on top, too, if wished.

HAKE WITH BACON, PEAS, AND CIDER

With its firm juicy flesh and fine flavor, hake lends itself perfectly to this quick-casserole approach. It keeps softly bouncy after its gentle poaching in crisp cider, sweet peas, and salty bacon.

I use a shallow, enamelled cast iron pan for this, 10 inches in diameter and 2 inches deep, but all that matters is that the pan you use is heavy-based, its lid tight-fitting, and that it is wide enough for the peas not to be too heaped up nor for the fish fillets to sit too tightly packed on top of them.

It is not advisable to make ahead/store

1   Warm the olive oil over a medium heat in a heavy-based pan that comes with a lid – though you don't need it on yet – then stir in the bacon and cook for 5 or so minutes, or until it is crisped at the edges, turning golden brown in parts, and the fat has rendered. Turn the heat up and add the peas, stirring them in the bacon, so that the look of the freezer has left them slightly and they are glossed in bacon fat.

2   Pour in the cider and let it come to a boil, then turn the heat down a little so that the cider simmers enthusiastically for about 5 minutes until the peas are cooked. They will have lost their bright green color, but that's how it should be. Taste to see if you need to salt; this will depend on how salty the bacon is.

3   Add the fish, skin-side down, to the pan of peas and bacon, put on the lid, and leave to simmer, now a little less excitedly – so keep an eye on the heat – for 10 minutes, or until just cooked through. Check to see if the fish is cooked in the center: I push a sharp knife through the side. If there is still a little pinkness within, put the lid back on, but turn off the heat, and let the fish stand and finish cooking tenderly in the residual heat for 5 minutes, or until just cooked through.

4   Transfer each fish fillet, skin-side down, to the center of a dinner plate, then sprinkle a little sea salt and grind some pepper over. Stir most of the parsley into the peas and bacon in the pan, then arrange around the fish, in slightly retro fashion. Spoon the cidery juices over each fillet and sprinkle the remaining parsley on top.

SERVES 2

Regular olive oil – 2 teaspoons
Bacon – 6 slices, snipped into approx. ¼ inch strips
Frozen petits pois – 1½ cups
Dry hard cider – 1 cup
Sea salt flakes or kosher salt – to taste
Hake or cod fillets – 2 thick, skin-on (approx. 7 ounces each)
Pepper – a good grinding
Italian parsley – ¼ cup finely chopped leaves

POLENTA-FRIED FISH
WITH MINTED PEA PURÉE

This is the perfect British "fish and chip shop" supper, or at least my play on it. The fish isn't battered – nor deep-fried, you may be relieved to hear – but coated in a golden mixture of fine polenta and turmeric, which gives a thin crust with a lot of crunch. Even if that makes the fish look like it's been dredged in garish dyed bread crumbs out of a package, it certainly doesn't taste like it. Besides, I've always had a weakness for a culinary visual pun.

The traditional accompaniment of "mushy peas" is represented by a sweetly garlicky minted pea purée, and some crushed baby potatoes, roasted until a crisp golden brown before being generously sprinkled with sea salt flakes and splashed exuberantly with raw unfiltered apple cider vinegar, stand in for the chips (see p.127).

For make ahead/store notes see p.276

1   Mix the polenta and turmeric in a dish big enough to dredge the fish in, then get out another, similar-sized dish, crack the egg in it, and whisk with the salt. Get out a cutting board or baking sheet and cover with a piece of parchment paper.

2   Dip each fish fillet, in turn, on both sides in the egg wash, making sure they are well coated, then do the same in the dish of polenta so that the fillets are well covered and no white bits show through. Transfer to your prepared board, skin-side down, and leave to set and dry out a little while you get on with the pea purée.

3   Heat the butter and oil in a small saucepan over a medium-low heat, add the garlic, and cook, stirring for a couple of minutes, pushing down on it with your spoon to break it up a bit while you do so. Tip in the frozen peas, turn the heat up, and stir the peas in the garlicky butter. Add the salt and freshly boiled water just to cover.

4   Strip the mint leaves from their stalks, put the leaves to one side, and drop the stalks into the pan of peas. Bring to a boil, then turn down the heat a little and leave the peas to cook, uncovered, at a robust simmer for about 10 minutes until the peas are tender, then turn off the heat. Using the pan lid to stop the peas tumbling out, strain the liquid out into a bowl and add 3 tablespoons back into the pan. Pick out the mint stalks from the peas and discard, then add the sour cream. Roughly tear the set-aside mint leaves and drop

SERVES 2

For the fish:
Polenta (not instant) – ½ cup
Ground turmeric – 1 teaspoon
Egg – 1 large
Fine sea salt – 1 teaspoon
Cod fillets or other firm white fish – 2, skin-on (approx. 7 ounces each), cut from the tail end
Vegetable oil – approx. 3 cups, or enough to give about a ½ inch layer in a large frying pan

For the pea purée:
Unsalted butter – 2 tablespoons
Regular olive oil – 1 teaspoon
Garlic – 1 fat clove, bruised and slightly splintered with the flat side of a wide-bladed knife, then slipped out of its skin
Frozen petits pois – 2⅓ cups
Sea salt flakes or kosher salt – 1 teaspoon
Water from a freshly boiled kettle – approx. 1 cup
Mint – 4 leafy sprigs
Sour cream – 2 tablespoons

To serve:
Salt and Vinegar Potatoes (see p.127)
Watercress

them in, then, with an immersion blender, blitz to a rough purée. Leave covered on the stove while you get on with frying your fish.

5   Pour vegetable oil to a depth of ½ inch into a frying pan large enough to take the fish fillets without crowding them; I use one of 12 inches diameter. Warm over a medium-high heat until hot but not smoking. This may seem a lot of oil, but if you use less, the fish will get greasy; the hot, ever more golden oil that bubbles up around the fish helps seal it as it cooks. Fry the polenta-crusted fillets for about 2 minutes each side, skin-side down first, by which time the grainy coating will be crisp, its goldenness deepened and darkened a little, and the fish cooked, but do check. Carefully lift the fish out of the pan and place, skin-side down, on two waiting plates.

6   Dollop the pea purée on each plate, alongside the fish and serve – for full effect – with the Salt and Vinegar Potatoes on p.127 and, should you so wish, a tangle of watercress.

SALT AND VINEGAR POTATOES

Baby white potatoes – 1 pound

Regular olive oil – 3 tablespoons

Raw unfiltered apple cider vinegar – 2½ teaspoons, or to taste

Sea salt flakes or kosher salt – 1½ teaspoons, or to taste

While steaming then roasting potatoes may seem rather a fandango, one bite of these will convince you that it's utterly worth it; besides, it's not as if you have do anything while they either steam or roast.

If you're making these to go with the Polenta-Fried Fish with its Minted Pea Purée on p.122, just make sure these are in the oven first. And don't start frying the fish before the potatoes are on their final furlong. But don't feel confined to this partnership: they're out of this world with a fried egg; though I can eat them with anything or, frankly, by themselves.

Go slowly when adding the salt and vinegar, tasting as you go, as I like these to have the wincing hit of salt and vinegar chips, and you may prefer a lighter hand with the sprinkling.

For make ahead/store notes see p.276

1   Steam the potatoes until tender (this takes 20–30 minutes). When cooked, turn off the heat, pour off the water from the saucepan below the steam pan, then sit the perforated pan on top of the empty, hot saucepan with the lid off to dry the potatoes. If it makes your life easier, you can steam the potatoes a couple of hours in advance as it would be fine roasting them once they're cooled, so long as they haven't been in the fridge.

2   Preheat the oven to 425°F, then pour the oil into a small, shallow roasting pan and heat it in the oven for 5 minutes.

3   Tip the potatoes out onto a plate, and crush with a fork, but not too thoroughly. You want some of them crumbling into small pieces, but mostly think of more or less halving, leaving rough edges, the better to crisp and brown in the oven.

4   Take the roasting pan out of the oven, carefully turn the potatoes in the oil, and then roast for 20 minutes, then turn them and cook for a further 10 minutes until they are a deep golden brown in parts and the rough edges are crisp; the smaller pieces will be dark and crunchy.

5   Remove to a serving bowl and sprinkle with vinegar and salt, then taste one of the potatoes – ultimate sacrifice – to see if you need to add more of either.

ROAST LOIN OF SALMON
WITH ALEPPO PEPPER AND FENNEL SEEDS

SERVES 2–3

Regular olive oil – 1 tablespoon
Loin fillet of salmon – approx. 1 pound, skinless, cut from the top end
Aleppo pepper/Turkish red pepper flakes – ½ teaspoon
Fennel seeds – 1 teaspoon
Sea salt flakes or kosher salt – to taste

To serve:
Salad leaves of your choice

Salmon loin is a cut that I'd normally think best suited to curing, but I've found this long fleshy fillet lends itself very well to brief, high-heat roasting. I like my salmon to veer toward undercooked, so that it keeps its coral-bellied interior, but this is not for everyone and, actually, even I like this when it's fully cooked through. The quick blitz in the hot oven seems to keep the flesh tender.

Aleppo pepper or Turkish red pepper flakes (see p.14) is one of my newfound enthusiasms and, in or out of the kitchen, happiness is best when shared. It's easy to find online, but if you can't get your hands on it, replace it with ¼ teaspoon of crushed red pepper flakes mixed with ¼ teaspoon of paprika and a little grated lemon zest.

This is best eaten warm rather than piping hot. And it's excellent cold, too.

For make ahead/store notes see p.276

1   Preheat the oven to 425°F.

2   Pour the oil into a small, shallow roasting pan, in which the salmon will fit fairly snugly (line it with aluminum foil if it isn't non-stick), then turn the salmon in it, leaving it skinned-side up. Sprinkle half the spices over, then turn the salmon the other way around and sprinkle with the remaining spices, now leaving it skinned-side down.

3   Cook in the hot oven for 8–10 minutes – just cut into it with the tip of a sharp knife to see if it's cooked enough for you. Once it's ready, sprinkle with salt and let it stand out of the oven for a minute or so, just so that the bold heat of the oven has left it, then break it roughly with a couple of forks into large pieces and arrange on a serving plate which you have lined first with the salad leaves of your choice.

COCONUT SHRIMP
WITH TURMERIC YOGURT

This is my version of a dish I fell in love with Stateside, and make greedily and contentedly back at home. The rice flour I dredge the shrimp in makes the coconut adhere much better than the more usual all-purpose flour, and it gives a crispness and light rustling crunch, in the same way the panko does, rather than regular bread crumbs, and both offer a more resilient coating, so that the encased shrimp steam succulently within.

For make ahead/store notes see p.276

1   Mix the yogurt, turmeric, and salt together and leave to stand so that the flavor mellows while you get a-frying.

2   Tip the rice flour into a shallow dish and put to one side, then beat the eggs and salt together in another similar dish. In a third shallow dish, mix the panko bread crumbs, coconut, and cayenne pepper.

3   Dredge a quarter of the shrimp in the rice flour, just to coat them lightly, and then drop them into the beaten eggs.

4   Lift them out and waggle them over the egg dish to let the excess drip off them a little, then add the shrimp to the panko and coconut mixture, getting your hands stuck in, and turning and pressing them into the mixture to make sure they are well coated. Put the shrimp on a baking sheet lined with parchment paper before dredging and dipping the remaining batches.

5   Set a mesh ladle or a slotted spoon as well as a large plate, lined with paper towels, near the stove. Pour the oil into a heavy-based saucepan of about 9 inches in diameter – any wider and you'll need a lot more oil – so that it comes about 1¼ inches up the sides of the pan, and heat it until a cube of bread sizzles when dropped in.

6   Fry a smallish batch of shrimp in the hot oil until crisp and golden, which shouldn't take more than a minute or so. Use the mesh ladle or slotted spoon to transfer them onto the paper towels.

SERVES 3–4, OR DOUBLE THAT IF PICKING AT THEM WITH A DRINK

For the sauce:
Coconut-milk yogurt – 1 cup
Ground turmeric – 1 teaspoon
Sea salt flakes or kosher salt – ½ teaspoon

For the shrimp:
Rice flour – ½ cup
Eggs – 2 large
Sea salt flakes or kosher salt – 1 scant teaspoon
Panko bread crumbs – 1 cup
Unsweetened shredded coconut – ¾ cup
Cayenne pepper – ½ teaspoon
Fresh raw shell-off large shrimp – 10 ounces (41–50 count/pound, approx. 34)
Vegetable oil – approx. 4 cups

7   Repeat with the other shrimp in similar-sized batches until you have cooked them all. Serve the turmeric yogurt in little bowls, one per eater, to dip into. Or just put into one bowl, with a spoon for people to dollop on their plates.

CHICKEN AND PEA TRAYBAKE

SERVES 4

Frozen petits pois – 7 cups (approx. 2 pounds)
Leeks – 4–5 medium-large, trimmed and cut into approx. 1 inch slices
Garlic – 2 fat cloves, peeled and minced
Dry white vermouth – ¼ cup
Regular olive oil – 2 tablespoons, plus more for drizzling
Sea salt flakes or kosher salt – 2 teaspoons, plus more for sprinkling
Dill – small bunch, torn into pieces
Chicken thighs – 8, skin-on and bone-in

I thought I had exhausted the culinary possibilities of a package of frozen peas, but my friend, and excellent cook, Alex Andreou, led me by the hand – it does take a leap of faith – to his method of using them, still frozen, as the first layer of a traybake. It's a life-changer. The peas become soft and sweet in the heat – duller in color, but so much more vibrant in flavor – and the steam they produce as they bake makes the chicken beautifully tender, its skin crackly and crisp on top.

What's key here is the size of the roasting pan. I wouldn't go any smaller – measuring from inside rim to inside rim – than about 15 × 11 inches (a little larger is fine) as there needs to be space around the chicken thighs for the magic to happen.

For make ahead/store notes see p.276

1   Preheat the oven to 400°F and clatter the frozen peas into a large roasting pan, followed by the leeks, garlic, vermouth, 2 tablespoons of oil, 2 teaspoons of salt, and most of the dill. Turn everything together in the pan – breaking up any large clumps of the frozen peas – until well mixed. I advise you to wear CSI gloves for this, just to stop you getting frostbite, though you still will feel the cold.

2   Arrange the chicken thighs, skin-side up, on top, then drizzle them with a little olive oil and give them a good sprinkling of salt, before roasting in the oven for 45 minutes. Remove from the oven, give the peas a small stir or tamp down, so that the few that are sitting on the surface and drying out a little are submerged in the liquid. Don't do the same to the leeks, however, as the bits that are peeking out will become desirably caramelized in the heat. Put back in the oven for a further 30 minutes, by which time the peas and leeks will be soft, and the chicken tender and cooked through, its skin golden and crisp.

3   Tear off the remaining dill fronds, and scatter over the top on serving, perhaps with some simply steamed baby potatoes to soak up the pea and chicken juices.

CHICKEN WITH RED GRAPES AND MARSALA

Brimming with mellow fruitfulness, the muskiness of the Marsala and the scented woodsiness of the thyme, this is the perfect autumnal supper; that said, it doesn't stop me eating this all year round.

If you're one of those people who keep homemade broth in ice cubes in the freezer – and reader, I was that person once – that's great, but I am happy to make this with store-bought chicken broth.

A chicken supreme is simply a skin-on chicken breast with the peg bone attached; it stays wonderfully juicy when cooked and gives depth to the sauce. You can use a regular chicken breast – so long as it still has its skin – though it won't be as plump, so will need a little less time in the oven.

It is not advisable to make ahead/store

SERVES 2

Marsala – ¼ cup
Chicken broth – ¼ cup
Dijon mustard – 1 teaspoon
Regular olive oil – 1 tablespoon
Chicken supremes – 2
Seedless red grapes – approx. 20
Thyme – approx. 1 tablespoon
of leaves, plus a few sprigs for sprinkling

To serve:
A baguette or baby white potatoes

1   Preheat the oven to 400°F and mix the Marsala, broth, and mustard together in a small bowl.

2   Heat the oil in a solidly made frying pan or shallow braiser or cast-iron skillet in which the chicken breasts will fit fairly snugly, and that will go on the stove and in the oven.

3   Fry the chicken supremes, skin-side down, for 5 minutes, by which time the skin will be golden. Turn the chicken skin-side up, add the Marsala mixture to the pan and let it quickly bubble up, then drop in the grapes and sprinkle in most of the thyme leaves. Bring back to a bubble, then transfer to the oven and cook for 20 minutes, or until the chicken skin is bronzed and crisp and the chicken itself just cooked through and wonderfully tender.

4   Transfer the chicken and grapes to two shallow bowls or dinner plates, then put the pan over a high heat, and let the juices bubble for 2–3 minutes, or until slightly reduced and thickened to a savory syrup. Pour around, but not over, the chicken. I know this sounds restaurant-fancy, but it's to keep the skin crisp. Scatter some leaves and delicate sprigs of thyme over, and serve, with perhaps a baguette to dip into the rich chickeny juices, or steam some baby white potatoes to have alongside.

LIME AND CILANTRO CHICKEN

I often, uncharitably, think that chicken breast fillet is the default choice of eating-averse fatphobes. I'm not sure I've ever looked down a restaurant menu and thought "Yes! That is just what I want." But I find ready zest for this. The supercharged acidity of the lime does double duty, tenderizing the meat beautifully and infusing it with fierce fragrance.

My plan of action – and one I recommend – is that you buy breasts with the skin still on. Remove the skin and fry it in a little oil for about five minutes each side, pressing down on it regularly, until it's a dark gold, has rendered its fat (keep this schmaltz for eating on toast at another time) and is crisping up. Remove to a plate lined with paper towels: it will become completely crisp as it cools. Tear up some iceberg lettuce – please, I've had just about as much as I can take of the insecure musings of salad snobs – and dress it lightly before crumbling in shards of the crisp chicken skin.

For make ahead/store notes see p.276

1   Remove the skin from the chicken and set this aside for now.

2   Cover a cutting board with plastic wrap, though do not cut off the piece from the roll quite yet, and sit the chicken breasts on top, with space between them, then cover with more plastic wrap and tear off from the roll. Using a rolling pin, press down on the meatier parts of the fillets, rolling them out a little, until each chicken breast is, as much as possible, of even thickness, though it's always going to be a little thinner at the tip. The idea is not to bash the chicken until it's a limp rag.

3   Put the lime zest in a small bowl, cover with plastic wrap, and set aside. Unwrap and transfer the chicken breasts to a resealable plastic bag, then add the lime juice along with the oil, salt, and garlic. Seal the bag well, give it a bit of a squidge to help it coat the chicken and leave to marinate, out of the fridge, for 15 minutes. While the chicken is marinating, you can be frying the chicken skins (see recipe introduction).

4   When time's up on the marinade, heat the 2 teaspoons of olive oil in a heavy-based frying pan. Take the chicken out of the bag and shake off the marinade before frying over a medium-high heat for 2 minutes each side, then turn again and give an extra minute on

SERVES 2

Chicken breast fillets – 2 (approx. 6 ounces each), preferably skin-on (see recipe introduction)
Lime – 1, finely grated zest and juice
Regular olive oil – ¼ cup, plus 2 teaspoons for frying
Sea salt flakes or kosher salt – ½ teaspoon
Garlic – 1 clove, peeled and minced
Cilantro – 2 tablespoons finely chopped leaves

To serve:
Iceberg lettuce
Avocado
Crushed red pepper flakes

each side, so that the chicken is bronzed on the outside and cooked through. Remove to a couple of waiting plates.

5   Mix the lime zest and chopped cilantro together and sprinkle on top. Serve, ideally, with the iceberg lettuce and chicken crackling and a splodge of avocado mashed with salt and red pepper flakes.

BUTTERFLIED CHICKEN
WITH MISO AND SESAME SEEDS

You can easily ask a butcher to butterfly the chicken for you, but it isn't difficult to do at home and can be curiously pleasurable. Just sit the chicken, breast-side down, on a board and press down a little until you hear a gratifying crunch. With a good pair of kitchen scissors or poultry shears, cut along each side of the backbone. Remove the backbone, then flip the chicken over and press down on the breast, to flatten it a little.

The marinade infuses the chicken overnight with a deep and musky saltiness, but not spikily so; intense though miso most definitely is, it works subtly, bringing its caramelly saltiness to the meat. This is much recommended with sushi rice and the Bashed Cucumber and Radish Salad on p.98.

For make ahead/store notes see p.276

For make ahead/store notes see p.276

SERVES 4–6

Vegetable oil – 1 tablespoon
Asian sesame oil – 2 teaspoons
White miso – 4 teaspoons
Soy sauce – 1 tablespoon
Fish sauce – 2 teaspoons
Fresh ginger – 1 tablespoon finely grated
Garlic – 1 fat clove, peeled and minced
Chicken – 1 (approx. 4 pounds), butterflied (see recipe introduction)
Sesame seeds – 2 teaspoons

1   Mix the vegetable oil, 1 teaspoon of the sesame oil, miso, soy sauce, fish sauce, ginger, and garlic in a small bowl.

2   Put the butterflied chicken into a large resealable plastic bag, pour in the contents of the bowl, and then carefully seal the bag. Turn the bag over a couple of times, squidging it as you do so, to make sure the chicken is covered with the marinade. Place the bag in a dish and sit it in the fridge to marinate overnight.

3   An hour or so before you want to roast the chicken, take the bag out of the fridge and tip it out, marinade and all, into a shallow roasting pan, sitting the chicken breast-side up. Leave to come to room temperature.

4   Preheat the oven to 400°F. Cover the chicken with aluminum foil before putting in the oven for 45 minutes.

5   Take the chicken out of the oven and remove the foil. Baste with some of the pan juices then drizzle the remaining teaspoon of sesame oil over the chicken and sprinkle over the sesame seeds. Put back in the oven, uncovered, for another 20 minutes, by which time the skin should be burnished, the chicken cooked through, and the juices caramelized.

6   Cut into quarters, or completely joint the chicken if you want it to serve more than 4, and pour the dark golden pan juices over the top.

INDIAN-SPICED CHICKEN AND POTATO TRAYBAKE

SERVES 6

Potatoes – 3¼ pounds, peeled and cut into approx. 1 inch cubes

Cumin seeds – 2 teaspoons

Fennel seeds – 2 teaspoons

Yellow mustard seeds – 2 teaspoons

Nigella seeds – 2 teaspoons

Ground turmeric – ½ teaspoon

Limes – 2, finely grated zest and juice

Garlic – 4 cloves, peeled and minced

Sea salt flakes or kosher salt – 2 teaspoons, plus more for sprinkling

Cold water – ¼ cup

Chicken thighs – 12, skin-on and bone-in

Regular olive oil – 2 tablespoons

To serve:
Cilantro
Quick-pickled onions (see recipe introduction)

I am not one for peeling potatoes if I can get away without, but here you want the cubes of potato to drink in the spiced lime and chicken juices as they cook, becoming soft and almost soused.

You need eat nothing more with this than a good bitter-leaved salad. I'm always keen on an escarole, but a ruby mound of radicchio and a small bowl of Bollywood-pink, quick-pickled onions are just clamoring to be put on the table alongside. Simply squeeze the juice of 2–3 limes over 1 small red onion, peeled and cut into thin half-moons. Cover and let it steep while you prepare and cook the chicken. Lift the onions out of the marinade to serve.

And should you have any chicken left over, you can make one of my favorite sandwiches. Just mix together a tablespoonful of mayo, a pinch of salt, and a teaspoon each of mango chutney and garam masala, then shred and stir in the meat from one chicken thigh and clamp between two slices of bread.

For make ahead/store notes see p.276

1   Preheat the oven to 425°F. Put the cut potatoes into a large, shallow roasting pan and sprinkle with the spices, followed by the lime zest and juice, garlic, 2 teaspoons of salt, and the water.

2   Tumble the chicken into the pan, and toss everything well together then turn the chicken skin-side up on top of the potatoes. Drizzle the skin with the oil and sprinkle over a little salt, then cook in the oven for 1 hour, or until the potatoes are tender and the chicken cooked through, its skin golden and crisp. Serve scattered with chopped cilantro and, if wished, the quick-pickled onions.

CHICKEN BARLEY

SERVES 4–6

Leeks – 2 medium, trimmed and sliced into approx. 1 inch logs

Carrots – 2 large, peeled and cut into chunky batons

Parsnips – 2 large, peeled and cut into very chunky batons

Pearl barley – 1 cup

Chicken thighs – 6, bone-in and skin-off (see recipe introduction)

Hot chicken broth – 6 cups

English mustard – 4 teaspoons

Italian parsley – leaves from a small bunch, roughly chopped, to give 1 cup loosely packed

This thick, creamy pottage, somewhere cozily between a stew and a slightly soupy, sticky risotto, offers instant comfort. This is the sort of food that gets left behind in the Instagram age: not pretty to look at, but gratifyingly reassuring to eat.

It's not hard to remove the skin from a clutch of chicken thighs, and you can fry it to make chicken crackling to be crunched as it is, or splintered into a salad as on p.138. Nothing would go wrong if you were to keep the skin on but, for once, I prefer to keep the fat out of it. Do not even think about using boneless thigh fillets.

For make ahead/store notes see p.276

1   Tip the prepared vegetables into a heavy-based Dutch oven that comes with a lid, then add the barley and chicken thighs.

2   Pour the broth into a pitcher, stir in the mustard, then pour this over the contents of the pan. Bring to a boil – and this is when better-behaved cooks would tell you to skim off the frothy bits that rise to the top but, frankly, I'm too lazy to – then turn down the heat, partially cover and let simmer for 1 hour, though check every now and again to make sure it's not bubbling away too much or dolefully not enough, giving a stir as you do so. If it looks as if it's boiling dry, then pour in a little boiling water.

3   Once the hour's up, the barley, vegetables, and chicken should be tender and the juices all but absorbed. Not that a little soupiness would be the end of the world. Remove from the heat and let stand with the lid off for 10 minutes.

4   If you haven't used skinless thighs, remove and discard the chicken skin. Using a couple of forks, pull the meat off the bones, and discard the bones (my particular treat is to chew the cartilage off them before chucking them away, but it's not to everyone's taste). Then throw in some of the chopped parsley and stir it through the stew, and put the rest on the table for people to sprinkle over their own bowls as they eat. It probably goes without saying that if you're feeding small children, predisposed to be pernickety about Green Bits, then you would be ill-advised to stir any parsley into the stew.

ROAST CORNISH HENS
WITH COUSCOUS, CUMIN, CINNAMON, AND THYME STUFFING

While I'm not sure I'd want to have to stuff these small birds in any number, this is easy work when there's only a couple of you eating. The aromatic stuffing gives an almost medieval-feast richness to the delicate meat of the Cornish hens and, simple though this is to cook, there is something about having a whole plump golden bird to oneself that makes it feel like a mini banquet.

It is not advisable to make ahead/store

1   Take the Cornish hens out of the fridge in good time to let them lose their chill. You don't want to stuff them when they're too cold.

2   Put the couscous into a small bowl, stir in the cumin seeds, mint, dried thyme, cinnamon, turmeric, 1 teaspoon of salt, the finely grated lemon zest, and apricot confetti, before pouring over the 7 tablespoons of boiling water. Use a fork to mix, then cover the bowl with a plate and leave for 10 minutes.

3   While you're waiting, preheat the oven to 400°F. When time's up on the couscous, remove the plate, add the scallion, along with the pine nuts and a third – which is to say, a teaspoon – of the butter. Use a fork to mix everything together and help the butter melt into the couscous. Taste to see if you want to add any more salt.

4   Untruss the Cornish hens, if indeed they are trussed, and stuff them with the aromatic couscous, tamping down as you go. You need to leave a little space at the end of the cavity as the filling will swell a bit, and you don't want it to spill out as it cooks.

5   Put the Cornish hens in a small shallow roasting pan, smear them with the remaining butter, and roast for 40–45 minutes until cooked through and the stuffing is piping hot. Transfer to a couple of (preferably warmed) dinner plates. Add a little just-boiled water to the scant meat juices in the pan, and stir, scraping up any sticky bits from the bottom of the pan, until smooth. Pour over the proudly plump Cornish hens, then sprinkle with thyme.

SERVES 2

Cornish hens – 2 (approx. 1 pound each)

Whole wheat couscous – ¼ cup

Cumin seeds – 1 teaspoon

Dried mint – 1 teaspoon

Dried thyme – ½ teaspoon

Ground cinnamon – ¼ teaspoon

Ground turmeric – ¼ teaspoon

Sea salt flakes or kosher salt – 1 teaspoon, plus more to taste

Lemon – 1, finely grated zest

Soft dried apricots – 2, snipped into small pieces

Water from a freshly boiled kettle – 7 tablespoons, plus more for deglazing the roasting pan

Scallion – 1, halved lengthways then thinly sliced across

Pine nuts – 2 tablespoons, toasted

Unsalted butter – 1 tablespoon, soft

Fresh thyme – a few delicate sprigs

To serve:
Endive or other bitter leaves

CHICKEN FRICASSÉE
WITH MARSALA, CHESTNUTS, AND THYME

This is what chicken fricassée says to me: my grandmother's apartment on a Monday evening, when the leftovers from Sunday's roast chicken would be warmed up with some sliced button mushrooms and coated in a thick and creamy béchamel sauce, to be eaten on top of a small, mounded pyramid of rice.

This, however, is not the old-school frick of chick: for one, I cook it all from scratch, so that the sauce, rather than merely draping the chicken, is flavored by it; button mushrooms are replaced with porcini; the sauce is made with broth rather than milk; and Marsala and thyme give bosky depth, very different from the muffling blandness of the traditional béchamel.

Not that you couldn't make this with leftover chicken. And you might well consider it, too, when thinking of how to use up that post-Thanksgiving turkey; certainly, the sweet, nubbly chestnuts offer seasonal support for this proposition. If you're starting with leftovers rather than afresh, then proceed as below but add the spiced flour in step 5 and add the cooked chicken (or turkey) to the sauce towards the end of the cooking time, making sure it's hot all the way through before serving.

While this is one of my absolute favorite things to eat, I admit it has a face only a mother could love.

For make ahead/store notes see p.277

SERVES 4

Marsala – ¾ cup
Dried porcini – ¼ cup
All-purpose flour – 5 tablespoons
Sea salt flakes or kosher salt – 1 teaspoon
Nutmeg – a good grating
Pepper – a good grinding
Boneless, skinless chicken thighs – 1 pound, cut into 1 inch pieces
Unsalted butter – 3 tablespoons
Regular olive oil – 1 teaspoon
Leek – 1 large, trimmed and thinly sliced
Thyme – 2 teaspoons of leaves, plus more to serve
Chicken broth – 2 cups, or more as needed
Ready-cooked chestnuts from a package, jar, or can – 1½ cups, broken and crumbled into pieces

To serve:
Basmati rice

1   Heat the Marsala and porcini in a very small saucepan and, as soon as it comes to a bubble, switch off and leave for no less than 10 minutes.

2   Tip the flour, salt, nutmeg, and pepper into a large resealable plastic bag, shake to mix, and then add the cut-up chicken pieces. Seal the bag and shake it around so the chicken pieces get a good dredging.

3   In a heavy-based saucepan or Dutch oven big enough to take the meat, vegetables, and liquid, and in which you can stir easily without splashing, melt the butter and oil over a medium heat, then add the sliced leek and cook, stirring frequently, for 4–5 minutes until just soft.

4   Drain the porcini through a strainer suspended over a pitcher or bowl, reserving the Marsala, and finely chop them.

5   To the spring-like greenness of the leeks, add the autumnally-toned mushrooms, along with the 2 teaspoons of thyme leaves, and stir well. Turn the heat up and add the dredged chicken pieces and any flour left in the bag. Give a good stir, until the flour is no longer visible in the pan, then add the mushroomy-Marsala and give another good stir before adding the chicken broth, followed by the chestnuts.

6   With the heat now turned down to medium, cook, stirring, for about 10 minutes until the sauce has thickened. Now, with the heat a little bit lower, cook for another 20 minutes, stirring every now and then to make sure the sauce is not catching at the bottom of the pan.

7   Check to make sure the chicken pieces are cooked through, adding some more chicken broth should the sauce have thickened too much. Serve with basmati rice and sprinkle with thyme.

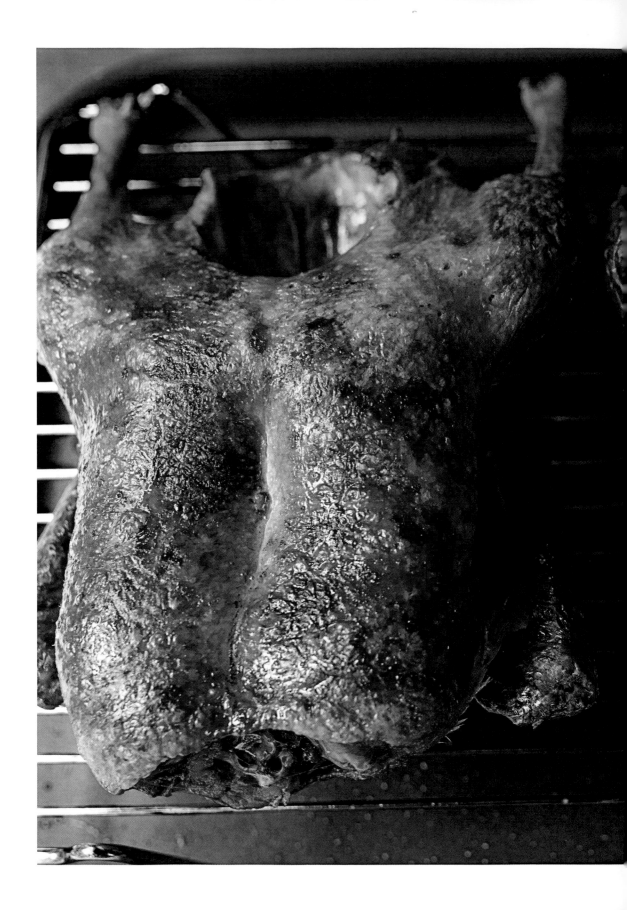

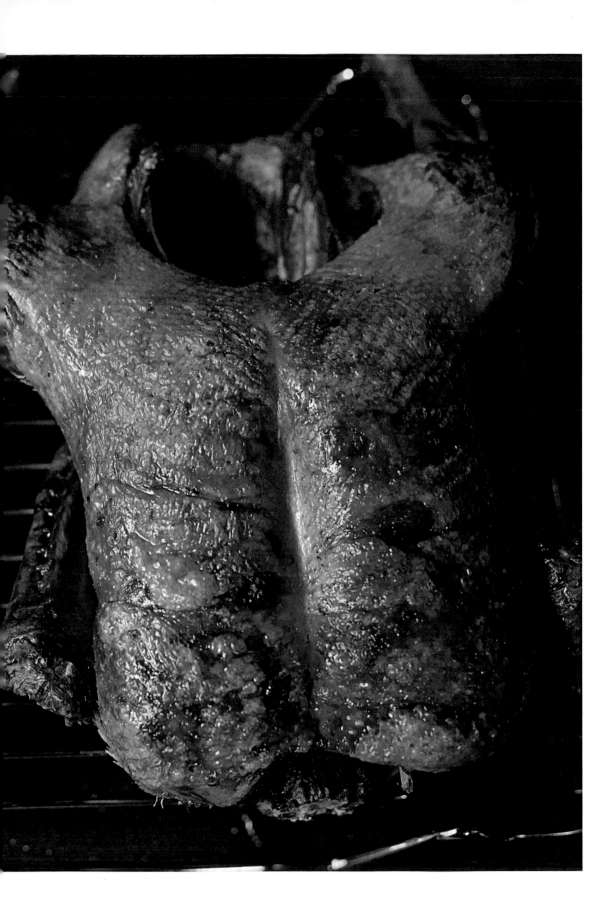

ROAST DUCK
WITH ORANGE, SOY, AND GINGER

The essence of a perfect roast duck is crisp skin and tender meat.
All too often, the former comes at the cost of the latter. I have been
assured that the platonic ideal of a roast duck can be achieved by
blanching it in boiling water three times; suspending it for a couple
of days on a clothes hanger to dry; inserting a straw under the skin
and blowing through it so that the skin puffs up and away from the
flesh; then hanging it vertically in the oven to roast. That's never
going to work for me.

But I have a method that does. It is a two-stage process, but
don't let that put you off, as both stages are very low-effort. In
fact, it's a development and simplification of a recipe from *How to
Eat*, in which the duck was poached, cooled, then roasted. There's

Ducks – 2 x 4½ pounds (or 4 pounds
without giblets)
Smooth-skinned oranges – 2
medium-sized, skin only, finely pared
with a vegetable peeler
Fresh ginger – 2 x 1½ inch pieces,
cut into coins
Star anise – 4
Cold water – 2 cups
Soy sauce – 5 tablespoons
Honey – 2 tablespoons

nothing wrong at all with that method, but it occurred to me that the same glorious effect could be achieved by steaming the duck in the oven, which does away with the need to get a duck in and out of a pot of bubbling water. The initial steam-roasting works in the same way, though: the meat cooks gently, and stays tender, and the excess fat under the skin drips away, which makes the skin itself crisp up more during its second-stage roasting. (It also means that the oven won't get as smoky as it does with any regular roasting method.) Despite the Asian-spiced sauce – more of an anointing liquid, really – this isn't in any way a Peking roast duck, with its lacquer carapace, but a perfect, plain roast duck with wonderful, wafery crisp skin and delicate shards of quackling.

You don't need to add anything to the duck as it roasts, as both meat and sauce deliver all the flavor needed. I say "duck" but we're actually talking ducks here, as you can't get enough for more than two or three people out of one.

I love this with no more than some plain rice and perhaps a Kaffe Fassett tapestry of cavolo nero. But for a festive roast, I bring out the Garlic and Parmesan Mashed Potatoes (p.66), Brussels Sprouts with Preserved Lemons and Pomegranate (p.76), and the Red Cabbage with Cranberries (p.72), even if the sauce is not quite in the same register; I have catholic tastes.

And going off on another tangent, leftovers are wonderful stirred into rice noodles or stuffed into soaked rice paper wraps; see the Cellophane Rolls on p.158.

For make ahead/store notes see p.277

1   Take the ducks out of the fridge. Remove and discard the giblets, if the ducks have come with them (or for a cook's treat, fry the liver in butter and deglaze with brandy), then cut off and discard the parson's nose with a pair of scissors and remove any excess fat around the cavity. Leave the ducks to come to room temperature. Lightly prick the skin all over with a toothpick.

2   Preheat the oven to 350°F. Once it's hot, pour water from a freshly boiled kettle into a deep roasting pan, to come about ½ inch up the sides, and place a rack on top. Sit the ducks on it, breast-side up, and cook in the oven for 1½ hours. Then take the pan carefully out of the oven and, again, prick the ducks assiduously: you will see the fat bubbling and running out. Using oven gloves for ease, remove

the ducks – pouring any liquid collected in the cavities into the pan below – to a couple of baking sheets, or similar, and leave to cool before transferring to the fridge (within 2 hours), where they can stay, preferably uncovered, for a day or two. Once it's cooled down a little, carefully pour the liquid from the roasting pan into a large, heatproof pitcher and leave to cool, then refrigerate. When the fat's cold and solidified, remove (discarding the water underneath) and store in the fridge to roast with at a later date.

3   About 2 hours before you want to roast your ducks, take them out of the fridge and sit them breast-side up, on top of a wire rack sitting over a deep roasting pan, to come to room temperature; they really mustn't have any chill about them. As soon as the ducks are out of the fridge, drop the finely pared orange peel into a small saucepan. Add the ginger, star anise, and cold water and bring to a boil. Let it boil for 1 minute, then turn off the heat and leave to steep for 2–3 hours.

4   Preheat the oven to 425°F. Lightly prick the duck skin all over with a toothpick, yet again, and if you're lucky you'll see a few fatty blisters, bubble-wrap style, probably on the underside: if you do, press on them to push out and remove little dots of fat; this is very satisfying work. I know it doesn't sound attractive in the context of cooking, but I have to say it: it is just like squeezing spots.

5   Transfer the ducks to the hot oven and roast for 50–60 minutes, turning the pan around halfway through, until the skin is crisp and bronzed. You will get some stippled dark brown patches – that's fine. Remove from the oven and let stand for 10 minutes.

6   Before you carve, finish the sauce. Remove and discard the orange peel, ginger, and star anise. Add the soy sauce, put the pan back on the heat and bring to a boil, then switch off the heat and stir in the honey to dissolve it. Pour into a warmed gravy boat or pitcher.

7   Carve the breast thinly and remove the meat from the legs or leave them whole as wished, then arrange on a warmed plate, along with any crisp skin that's left on the bird. Spoon a little of the orange, soy, and ginger sauce just over the meat. Serve absolutely immediately.

CELLOPHANE ROLLS

I have Zoe Wales to thank for this perfect suggestion for using up leftovers of the Roast Ducks on p.154. And just as, when hot, the ginger, orange, and soy broth makes for a beautifully flavored gravy, cold it serves as an excellent dipping sauce.

    I have two things in particular to say about this recipe. First, while rather easy to do, it is relatively complicated to explain how to do it. Just hold on to the fact that you're simply filling some wraps, then rolling them up. Second, you don't need to wait until you have leftover duck to make these. You could substitute whatever you wanted (some leftover 5-Spice Lamb, see p.160, or indeed any cold meat or fish, or a little chopped up avocado). If you're not starting off with the leftover Orange, Soy, and Ginger sauce, then substitute with 2 tablespoons of light soy sauce, add ½ teaspoon of lime juice to the lime zest, and 2 tablespoons of chopped Thai basil to the herbs when making the rolls, and use light soy sauce with a little fresh ginger grated into it for the dipping sauce.

It is not advisable to make ahead/store

1   Soak and drain the rice vermicelli following the package instructions, then tip the plumped-up translucent threads into a bowl and give a bit of a snip with a pair of scissors. This just makes the rolls easier to eat later.

2   Add the 2 tablespoons of Orange, Soy, and Ginger sauce and the fish sauce and toss to mix with a couple of forks. Then do the same with the lime zest, mint, cilantro, cucumber, scallions, and duck.

3   Soak the rice-paper wrappers one by one, again following the package instructions, and put each soaked wrapper, as you go, on a slightly dampened clean tea towel in front of you. Arrange about 2 heaping tablespoons of vermicelli-duck mixture in a straggly line across the wrapper, about 1 inch away from the edge nearest you. Fold that short edge over the filling, then give another roll to make it secure. Bring up the left and right sides of the wrapper and fold them over, then carry on rolling until you have a ghostly sausage in front of you. Do the same with the remaining 7 wrappers.

4   Serve with the dipping sauce.

MAKES 8 ROLLS

Rice vermicelli – 2 ounces
Orange, Soy, and Ginger sauce, leftover from p.154 – 2 tablespoons (or see recipe introduction)
Fish sauce – 1 teaspoon
Lime – 1, finely grated zest
Mint – ¼ cup roughly chopped leaves
Cilantro – ¼ cup roughly chopped leaves
English cucumber – ⅓ (approx. 2 ounces), seeded and cut into skinny batons
Scallions – 3, thinly sliced
Cold duck, leftover from p.154 – 1 cup, very finely shredded (or see recipe introduction)
Rice-paper wrappers – 8

To serve (as a dipping sauce):
Orange, Soy, and Ginger sauce, leftover from p.154 (or see recipe introduction)

SLOW ROASTED 5-SPICE LAMB
WITH CHINESE PANCAKES

Some friends told me about a year ago that they'd gone to a Chinese restaurant and, instead of having duck in pancakes, they'd had soft, shredded lamb. I became obsessed. I thought about it constantly. I endlessly imagined what it had tasted like. I dreamt of it. Enough! I just I had to cook it. I did. And then I didn't stop. I think by now I could stir up the 5-spice mixture and get this in the oven in my sleep. But then, it is very, very easy.

Of course, I don't make my own Chinese pancakes. For that matter, I'm told Chinese restaurants don't either. Though please don't feel confined to eating the lamb this way; it's good bundled into lettuce wraps, too. And I wouldn't rest easy in myself if I didn't tell you as well that the spiced, sweet and tangy meat – consider it pulled lamb – is also divine squished warm into bread rolls. Last of all, any leftovers are great with rice, along with the cooking juices I've kept expressly for this purpose.

For make ahead/store notes see p.277

1   Take the lamb out of the fridge for about an hour to come to room temperature and preheat the oven to 325°F. Line a roasting pan in which the lamb will sit snugly with a large piece of aluminum foil big enough to wrap around the lamb. Then place another large piece of foil on top, but in the opposite way to the first, giving you 4 ends of foil ready to make a parcel for your lamb.

2   Mix the ginger, 5-spice, vinegar, soy sauce, and 2 tablespoons of the honey together.

3   Put the lamb skin-side down on the foil-lined pan, and slash into the flesh with a sharp knife. Pour about half of the spice mixture over it, and massage it in well (you might want to think of wearing CSI gloves for this), then turn the lamb over, slash the skin side, and pour the rest of the spice mixture over, again massaging a little to try and help it get into the meat. Bring up the sides of the foil, to make a loose parcel, and scrunch together to seal tightly, then roast in the oven for 3½ hours.

4   Remove the pan from the oven, unwrap the foil, pulling down the sides so that you can spoon or ladle the juices into a bowl or pitcher, which is quite a boring job, but not a hard one. (Set these juices aside. When they're cold, refrigerate, then remove the fat. You can

SERVES 4–6

Lamb shoulder – bone-in, approx. 3½ pounds
Fresh ginger – 1 tablespoon finely grated
Chinese 5-spice – 4 teaspoons
Rice wine vinegar – 3 tablespoons
Soy sauce – 2 tablespoons
Honey – 3 tablespoons

To serve:
Chinese rice (or moo shu) pancakes – approx. 20
Iceberg lettuce – separated into leaves to use as wraps
Hoisin sauce
Scallions – cut into thin strips
English cucumber – seeded and cut into thin strips
And see recipe introduction, too

warm these up to reheat any leftover meat to eat with rice later.)
Pour the remaining tablespoon of honey over the top of the lamb,
and put back into the oven, uncovered, for a further 20 minutes,
at which time it will have a barbecue-blackened soft crust. Let it
stand out of the oven for 10 minutes.

5   Shred the meat – I just use a couple of serving forks – and transfer
    to a warmed wide bowl or platter. Eat in Chinese pancakes or
    lettuce wraps, along with some hoisin sauce and strips of scallion
    and cucumber.

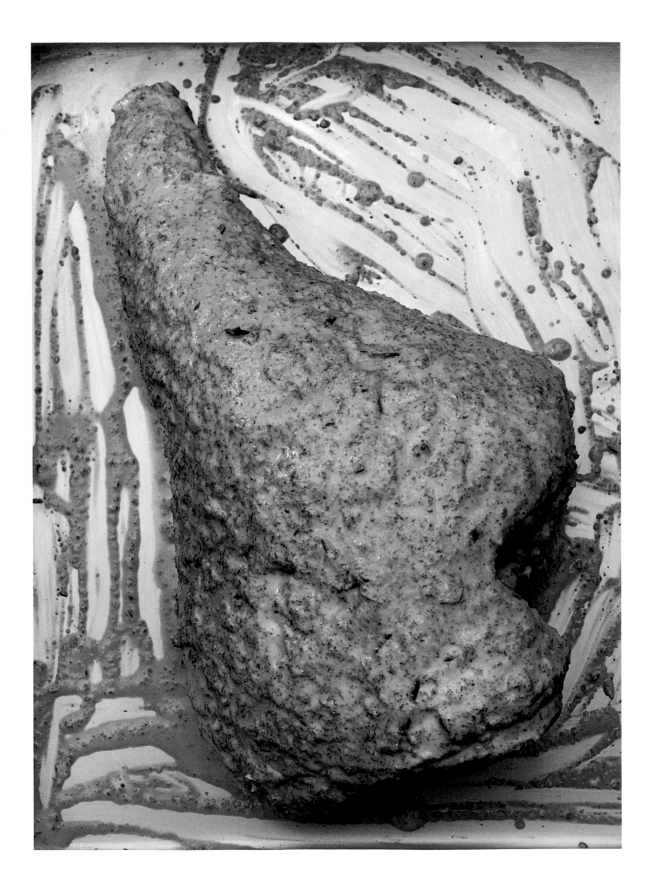

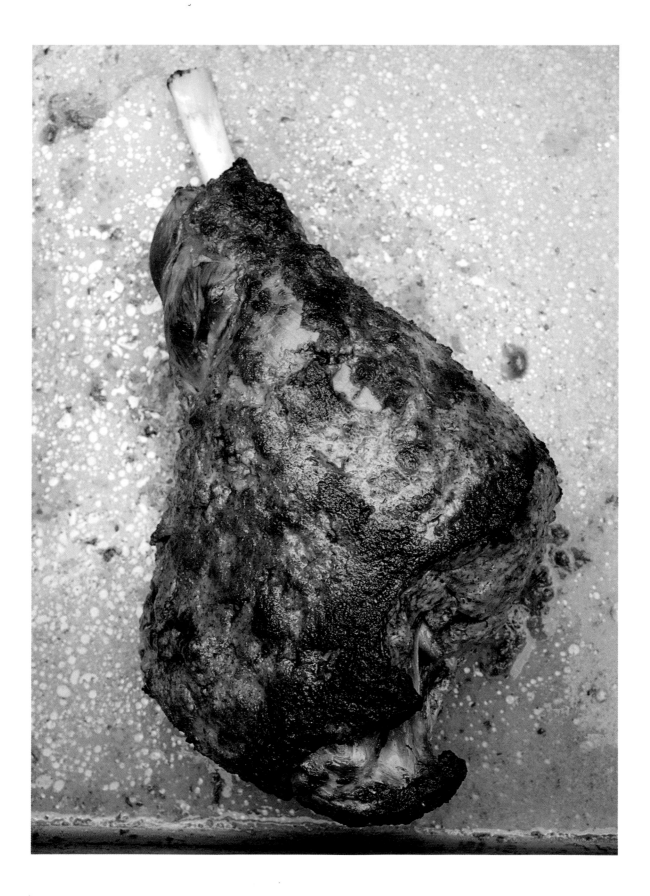

HERBED LEG OF LAMB

Recipes come into being in strange ways. The fabulous Brazilian pit master and chef, André Lima de Luca, told me about a way he had for slow-cooking a shoulder of pork with (among many other ingredients) oregano, rosemary, orange, and lemon. The thought and flavors percolated at the back of my mind for a while – and then I tried cooking a leg of lamb with them last Easter.

It's relaxingly simple to make: a quick blitz with an immersion blender, and you have an upliftingly fragrant, gloriously green paste which you coat the lamb with before roasting and, once cooked, gives a soft, fresh-flavored crust.

The timing below is based on your cooking a 3½ pound leg for 18 minutes per pound plus 20 minutes, which will give you medium, that's to say, pink lamb; if you want well-cooked lamb, then give it 27 minutes per pound plus 30 minutes. However, ovens do vary, and it's wise to use a temperature probe. I resisted for a long time, but now I get my probe out at every possible opportunity. But I don't cook the meat to the temperature that I want it to be (for pink lamb, that would be 140°F; for well done, 160°F) because I find that the meat carries on cooking as it rests, and I'm always nervous of overcooking it. If you want your meat well-done, then this isn't going to be a worry, but for pink meat I suggest that you take the lamb out when it reads 130°F, and rest it, covered loosely in aluminum foil, out of a draft for 15–30 minutes, testing with your probe to make sure you don't carve it until it's as you want it. But keep an eye, so it doesn't go over, either.

You don't exactly get a gravy out of the liquid at the bottom of the pan (the water stops the pan from burning and keeps the meat gorgeously tender) but taste it once the lamb's rested, to see if you want to add a little freshly boiled water, and possibly a drop or two of honey, to give you some juices to pour over the carved meat. If it's old-school gravy you're after, then I refer you to the orangey and lemony Cumberland Gravy on p.166.

For make ahead/store notes see p.277

SERVES 6–8

Leg of lamb – bone-in, approx. 3½ pounds
Oregano – leaves from a small bunch, to give ¾ cup loosely packed
Rosemary – 1 tablespoon needles
Garlic – 4 fat cloves, peeled and halved
Lemon – 1, finely grated zest and 2 tablespoons of juice
Orange – 1, finely grated zest and 2 tablespoons of juice
Regular olive oil – 2 tablespoons
Sea salt flakes or kosher salt – 2 teaspoons

1   Sit the lamb in a roasting pan, skin-side up, and make many plunging incisions all over the skin side with the tip of a sharp knife.

2   With an immersion blender, blitz the oregano, rosemary, garlic, lemon, and orange zests and juices, olive oil, and salt to a herb-flecked

runny paste. Pour or spoon this over the lamb and use your fingers to help get it into the meat where you've made your incisions. A lot of the paste will run off down into the pan: rub this into the sides, where the meat is exposed, and spoon over the top on the skin. Leave for 45 minutes or so until the lamb is at room temperature. Preheat the oven to 350°F.

3   Pour enough just-boiled water to come up about ¼ inch in the pan, and roast for 1 hour 40 minutes, though take a look at it after an hour or so to make sure that the water hasn't evaporated (if it has, add more) and the top isn't burning – if it is, cover loosely with aluminum foil – though it should, by the end of its cooking time, be darkened in places. I have never found it to burn in my oven, but some ovens are fiercer than others.

4   Before the time is quite up, remove from the oven and put your probe in, if you have one (see recipe introduction for notes and numbers). Otherwise pierce with a knife and peek in.

5   Remove the cooked lamb from the oven, cover loosely with foil, and let rest for 15–30 minutes, checking on it every now and again, before transferring to a board to carve.

CUMBERLAND GRAVY

This is an onion gravy, infused with the flavors of a Cumberland sauce, that appears on my table with, for my family, reassuring regularity.

For make ahead/store notes see p.277

1   Warm the oil in a heavy-based saucepan that comes with a lid, and stir in the onions. Cook, uncovered, over a medium heat for 10 minutes, checking regularly to make sure the onions aren't burning underneath; if they are beginning to, give them a good stir. Turn the heat to low, and give them another 7–10 minutes, checking and stirring regularly as before, until the onions are soft and golden. Add the red currant jelly and mustard, and stir until the jelly has melted into the onions.

2   Turn the heat up to medium again, and stir in the flour. Once it's mixed into the onions, gently pour in the port, orange juice, lemon juice, and broth, giving the pan another good stir. Now turn the heat to high to bring everything to a boil, stirring to get rid of any lumps.

3   Once the gravy's boiling, turn the heat to low, clamp on the lid, and leave to simmer for 15 minutes, lifting the lid to give it an occasional stir during this time. Taste for seasoning before pouring into a warmed gravy boat.

MAKES APPROX. 2½ CUPS

Regular olive oil – 2 tablespoons
Onions – 2 medium, peeled and cut into fine half-moons
Red currant jelly – 1 tablespoon
Dijon mustard – 1 teaspoon
All-purpose flour – 1 tablespoon
Ruby port – 5 tablespoons
Orange – 1 tablespoon of juice
Lemon – 1 teaspoon of juice
Chicken broth – 2 cups

LAMB KOFTA
WITH GARLIC SAUCE

These are rather like Eastern Mediterranean meatballs in sausage form, though you can come across them as fat burger-like patties, too. As loose-packed sausages, they're formed around skewers and turned over an open flame. Since I rarely use a barbecue, but just stare at it being rained on in the garden, I simply fry them in a pan. And much as I like the long lollipop approach, I can't make a skewer fit in the frying pan, so sausages – albeit highly seasoned and juicy sausages – it is.

I don't wish to be too prescriptive as to how you should eat them, but I roughly chop some tomatoes and parsley and mix them together in a bowl, to be brought to the table along with some shredded iceberg lettuce and an eye-poppingly intense garlic sauce. Eat them, hot-dog-style, wrapped in warm flatbreads.

For make ahead/store notes see p.277

1   Put all the kofta ingredients – barring the oil – into a large bowl and, with dampened hands and a light touch, mix everything together. While you need everything to be thoroughly combined, it's important not to make a dense, compact mixture.

2   Line a small baking sheet with plastic wrap, and form 2 heaped-tablespoons of the mixture into a sausage shape, then slightly flatten the sides as this will help them cook more evenly when you fry them. Transfer them onto the lined baking sheet as you go – you should get about 10 kofta.

3   Cover the baking sheet with plastic wrap and put in the fridge for about 30 minutes so that the kofta firm up a little. While you're waiting, stir the yogurt, garlic, lemon zest and juice, salt, and dried mint together. Your sauce is now made.

4   Heat the olive oil in a large frying pan and fry the kofta – over a highish heat – for 5 or so minutes each side until just cooked all the way through. Be gentle as you turn them over, so as not to break them up.

5   Serve with the garlic sauce, salad, and flatbreads, as wished.

SERVES 4–5

For the kofta:
Ground lamb – 1 pound
Onion – 1, peeled and coarsely grated, to give ¾ cup loosely packed
Garlic – 2 fat cloves, peeled and minced
Ground cumin – 1 teaspoon
Ground coriander – 1 teaspoon
Ground allspice – ¼ teaspoon
Ground white pepper – ½ teaspoon
Sea salt flakes or kosher salt – 1 teaspoon
Italian parsley – 3 tablespoons finely chopped leaves
Fresh mint – 3 tablespoons finely chopped leaves
Regular olive oil – 2 tablespoons

For the garlic sauce:
Plain whole milk Greek yogurt – 1⅔ cups
Garlic – 4 cloves, peeled and minced
Lemon – 1–2, finely grated zest of 1 and 3 tablespoons of juice
Sea salt flakes or kosher salt – 2 teaspoons
Dried mint – 2 teaspoons

To serve:
Tomatoes
Iceberg lettuce
Flatbreads

SPICED LAMB
WITH POTATOES AND APRICOTS

SERVES 6–8

Regular olive oil – ¼ cup

Onions – 2 medium, peeled and roughly chopped, to give 2 cups loosely packed

Cinnamon sticks – 1 long or 2 short

Garlic – 2 fat cloves, peeled and minced

Fresh ginger – 1 tablespoon finely grated

Ground cumin – 2 teaspoons

Ground coriander – 2 teaspoons

Ground allspice – 1 teaspoon

Smoked paprika – 1 teaspoon

Ground cloves – a pinch

Cardamom pods – 4–6, cracked open

Boneless lamb neck or leg – 2¾ pounds, diced for a stew

Potatoes – 2¼ pounds, peeled and cut into 1 inch chunks

Soft dried apricots – 1½ cups

Canned diced tomatoes – 1 x 14-ounce can

Cold water – 3 cups

Sea salt flakes or kosher salt – 2 teaspoons, or to taste

To serve:
Cilantro

This warmly aromatic lamb stew is just the sort of one-pot cooking that makes life easy when you have friends over; a traybake, which works on the same principle, being the other approach that dominates my cooking life. A bowl of green beans on the side and you're ready to go. Strictly speaking it's not necessary, but if you don't mind double-carbing (I'm all in favor of it), some whole wheat couscous on the table alongside is worth considering too. For this amount of stew, work along the lines of 2¾ cups couscous and 3¼ cups water, seasoning it as you wish, and perhaps stirring in some toasted sliced almonds at the end or, indeed, go with the Bulgur Wheat on p.177.

For make ahead/store notes see p.277

1   Preheat the oven to 325°F. Warm the oil in a large Dutch oven or ovenproof saucepan that has a lid over a medium heat, then add the onions and cinnamon stick (or sticks). Cook gently for about 10 minutes, stirring every now and then. When the onions have softened and are beginning to color a little, add the minced garlic and ginger. Stir in the cumin, coriander, allspice, paprika, cloves, and cardamom pods.

2   Tip in the diced lamb and turn in the spiced oil, coating all the pieces well, then add the potatoes and turn them, too. Drop in the dried apricots, pour in the canned tomatoes, then swill the tomato can out with some of the water and tip it into the pan. Add the rest of the water, stir in the salt, and bring to a boil. Once it's bubbling, clamp on the lid and cook in the oven for 2 hours.

3   Check that the lamb is tender and, if not, return to the oven for another 15–30 minutes. Remove from the oven and let stand for 10 minutes, then give a good stir as this will break up the potatoes a little, thickening the sauce. Sprinkle with cilantro and serve in shallow bowls, scattering a little more cilantro over as you go.

SPICY MINT LAMB CHOPS
WITH A PRESERVED LEMON AND MINT SAUCE

Although not an instant dinner, this is nonetheless simple and speedy to make. You do need to marinate the lamb for 30 minutes or so, but you can pour yourself a glass of wine, sit back and enjoy it, then whizz up the mint sauce in the meantime.

Speaking of which, this is a simple, spontaneous reworking of the old-fashioned vinegary mint sauce my mother used to make, using ingredients from my kitchen now. Namely, I saw two preserved lemons left bobbing hopefully about in their jar, and thought this would be an excellent opportunity to use them up. It was: the preserved lemons' intense and scented sourness counters and enhances the mint perfectly.

For make ahead/store notes see p.277

1   Put the lamb rib chops into a resealable plastic bag and add the olive oil, finely grated zest and juice of the lemon, dried mint, red pepper flakes, salt, and minced garlic. Seal the bag and give a good squidge before marinating for 30–40 minutes, long enough for them to come to room temperature.

2   To make the sauce, put the mint, garlic, preserved lemons and juice, and half the oil into a bowl and patiently blitz with an immersion blender. When most of the leaves have been incorporated, pour in the remaining oil and blitz again, until you have a deep emerald, emulsified sauce. Taste to see if you want to add salt, though I find the preserved lemons give all the salinity you need, and I am an enthusiastic salter.

3   Heat a grill pan (my preference) or heavy-based frying pan, then lift the cutlets out of the marinade and cook them over a high heat – if you want them a little pink – for 2 minutes each side. But check and cook longer as needed.

4   Arrange the lamb cutlets on a plate, lined with the greenery of your choice. Serve with the fragrant, sharp mint sauce, drizzling some on the cutlets too, if you so wish.

SERVES 3–4

For the lamb:
French-trimmed lamb rib chops – 8
Regular olive oil – 7 tablespoons
Lemon – 1, finely grated zest and juice
Dried mint – 2 teaspoons
Crushed red pepper flakes – 1 teaspoon
Sea salt flakes or kosher salt – 1 teaspoon
Garlic – 2 cloves, peeled and minced

For the mint sauce:
Fresh mint – leaves from a medium bunch, to give 2 cups loosely packed
Garlic – 1 fat clove, peeled and sliced into 3
Preserved lemons – 2 small, quartered, plus 2 tablespoons of juice from the jar
Regular olive oil – ½ cup

To serve:
Leaves of your choice (I'm keen on pea shoots here)

LAMB SHANKS
WITH DATES AND POMEGRANATE MOLASSES

Rich, sumptuous, and celebratory, this is a real feast of a stew. The dark, molasses-like dates melt into what becomes a deep, intense gravy, but they don't overwhelm it with sweetness; the heady sourness of pomegranate molasses keeps it all in fragrant check. But if, when you taste it at the end of its cooking time, you feel you want a bit more acerbity, just squeeze in a little lime juice.

One shank per person is an undeniably munificent portion. While this is certainly no bad thing, you can make this feed double the number of people simply by making the stew in advance. Once it's cooled a little, pull the meat off the shanks, shred roughly with a couple of forks, and put it back in the pot. Leave to cool, refrigerate, and then reheat in an oven preheated to 400°F for an hour or so, until piping hot, and sprinkle with pomegranate seeds.

Either way, this is splendid with the Bulgur Wheat on p.177 or the Smashed Chickpeas on p.74. If you're stretching out the stew to feed 10 people, I wouldn't double the amount of bulgur wheat or chickpeas but, rather, add half quantities again.

For make ahead/store notes see p.277

SERVES 6 OR, IF MEAT IS
SHREDDED (SEE RECIPE
INTRODUCTION), 10

Lamb shanks – 6

Regular olive oil – 3 tablespoons

Onions – 2 large, peeled and roughly
chopped, to give 3⅓ cups loosely packed

Garlic – 4 fat cloves, bruised and
slightly splintered with the flat side of
a wide-bladed knife, then slipped out
of their skins

Carrots – 2 large, peeled and cut into
chunky slices on the diagonal

Ground cumin – 2 teaspoons

Ground coriander – 1 teaspoon

Ground cinnamon – 1 teaspoon

Ground allspice – 1 teaspoon

Ready-ground black pepper –
2 teaspoons

Sea salt flakes or kosher salt –
2 teaspoons

Rosemary – 2 teaspoons finely
chopped needles, plus more to sprinkle

Soft dried pitted dates – 1½ cups
(approx. 30 small, or 15 large, halved)

Chicken broth – 1¼ cups

Pomegranate molasses – 3
tablespoons

Lime – 1, to squeeze, if wished

To serve:

Pomegranate seeds

1   Preheat your oven to 300°F. Put the lamb shanks into a large bowl
and pour the olive oil over them, then turn and rub them well to
make sure the oil lightly coats all the meat.

2   Heat a wide, heavy-based Dutch oven or ovenproof pan that the
shanks can all fit in snugly, and which has a tight-fitting lid. Put
half the shanks in to brown over a medium-high heat. Once they
are lightly browned, after about 5 minutes, put the first 3 shanks
back into the bowl, and repeat with the remaining shanks.

3   Once all the lamb shanks are out of the pan, turn the heat down
to medium and fry the onions, garlic cloves, and carrots for another
5 minutes or so until they start to lose their crispness.

4   Stir in the spices, pepper, salt, and finely chopped rosemary, then tip
in the dates and pour in the chicken broth and pomegranate molasses.
Once you have stirred this all together and the pan is bubbling, sit
the shanks back in, scraping in any juices from the bowl, with the
meaty side mostly in the liquid. You will need to fit them in like a
jigsaw puzzle in a single layer. Don't worry that there isn't much
liquid in the pan; you don't want there to be or the sauce will be
too runny later.

5   Tear off a large piece of parchment paper and place it over the
top of the meat and tuck it in well before clamping on the lid.
Transfer immediately to the oven.

6   Cook for approximately 3 hours but check after 2½ hours whether
the lamb is tender. The meat on the bone should be quite soft
and starting to come away from the shank, so be gentle as you lift
them out of the pan. Arrange in a large, shallow bowl. Check the
rich liquid in the pan for seasoning, adding a little lime juice if you
want more sharpness, then spoon some of the dark sauce over each
shank and sprinkle with a little finely chopped rosemary. Pour the
rest of the thick fruity gravy around the shanks and, if you aren't
suffering from pomegranate seed fatigue, scatter glisteningly on top.

BULGUR WHEAT
WITH SLICED ALMONDS AND NIGELLA SEEDS

SERVES 6–8

Regular olive oil – 1 tablespoon

Lemon – 1, finely grated zest and a squeeze of juice

Dried thyme – 1 teaspoon

Coriander seeds – 1 teaspoon

Cumin seeds – 1½ teaspoons

Nigella seeds – 2 teaspoons

Bulgur wheat – 2⅓ cups

Cold water – 3 cups

Sea salt flakes or kosher salt – 2 teaspoons, plus more to taste

Sliced almonds – ¾ cup, toasted and cooled a little

Italian parsley – leaves from a small bunch, roughly chopped, to give 1 cup loosely packed

Aromatic and light, this is the perfect accompaniment to any rich, spiced stew; cold, it makes for a sensational salad. I always pray for leftovers.

For make ahead/store notes see p.277

1   Heat the oil in a heavy-based saucepan or Dutch oven that comes with a tight-fitting lid and stir the lemon zest, thyme, coriander, cumin, and nigella seeds in the warm oil for about 30 seconds.

2   Add the bulgur wheat and stir well. Pour in the water and add the salt, bring to a boil, then clamp on the lid, lower the heat, and cook very gently for 15 minutes, by which time the water should be absorbed and the grains soft. Then switch off the heat, cover the pan with a clean tea towel, clamp on the lid, and leave for 10 minutes. Using a fork, stir well to get rid of any clumps. Season to taste.

3   Tip into a large bowl, add a squeeze of lemon juice, most of the almonds and parsley, and toss to mix, then sprinkle over what's left.

SLOW ROASTED PORK SHOULDER
WITH CARAMELIZED GARLIC AND GINGER

As far as I'm concerned this is the easiest route to a lazy weekend feast. True, a little forethought is needed – the garlic needs to be roasted the day (or certainly several hours) before the pork – but because of the time the pork takes to cook, I always get it in the house the day before I want to eat it anyway. I just put the garlic in the oven when I stash the pork shoulder (uncovered, so the rind is exposed to the air) in the fridge.

Caramelizing the garlic gives it a sweet intensity, and turns it into a thick creamy paste, just ready to be mixed with the ginger, soy, and touch of vinegar and smeared inside the pork, infusing it with heady flavor as it roasts.

Because the pork takes 6½ hours to cook, this is definitely supper rather than lunch (unless you want to get up at the crack of dawn) but since you largely ignore it as it slowly roasts, this is all gratifyingly stress-free.

As far as I'm concerned, you can never have too much crackling, so I advise getting a separate piece of scored skin from the butcher as well. The pork, once cooked, can be left loosely covered with aluminum foil while you put the extra piece of skin in to cook for 30–40 minutes in the hot oven.

While I want no more than the cooking juices spooned over the carved meat on its serving plate, I am used to cooking for those who require gravy with pretty much everything. If that's how you feel, too, then I suggest you make a pitcherful of the Cumberland Gravy on p.166.

For make ahead/store notes see p.277

For make ahead/store notes see p.277

SERVES 6–8

Garlic – 2 heads
Pork shoulder – 5½ pounds, boneless and skin-on, skin scored
Fresh ginger – 1 tablespoon finely grated
Soy sauce – 2 tablespoons
Raw unfiltered apple cider vinegar – 1 tablespoon

1   Preheat the oven to 425°F. Cut off the tops of the 2 heads of garlic, so that you can just see the cloves peeking through, and sit each scalped head of garlic, cut-side up, on a piece of aluminum foil large enough for you to be able to pull up the ends and scrunch them together to form a parcel. Put both parcels in the hot oven and roast for 45 minutes, by which time the cloves will be soft and caramelized, then remove from the oven and leave to cool, still wrapped in their foil parcels – this could take up to 3 hours.

2   Then, 7½ hours before you want to eat (fair warning) take the pork out of the fridge for about an hour to get the chill off it, and preheat the oven to 300°F. While you wait, unwrap the two parcels

of garlic, and squeeze the bulbs to push the sticky caramelized cloves out into a bowl. Add the ginger, soy, and vinegar and mix together.

3   Sit the pork, skin-side up, in a roasting pan in which it will fit snugly and spread the garlic and ginger paste into the pocket where the bone was. If there's any residue left in the bowl, you can smear this gently around the sides, but make sure you don't let any get on the skin. Pour some freshly-boiled water into the bottom of the pan, just to cover the base by about ¼ inch. How much water you'll need obviously depends on the size of your pan. Roast in the oven for 5 hours.

4   After these 5 hours, gently baste the sides of the pork with the juices that have collected in the pan, then leave to roast for another hour.

5   Remove the roasting pan from the oven, and turn the oven up to 425°F. Patiently spoon the juices into a wide-necked heatproof pitcher (it's easier than trying to pour them off) and return the pork to the hot oven for 30 minutes until the skin has turned into glorious, crunchy cracklings.

6   Transfer the pork to a board, and if you want to slip in another piece of skin to make extra cracklings, leave the cooked pork shoulder loosely tented with foil while your extra piece of skin cooks. But if you're not going for that option, leave the pork to stand anyway, just while you spoon off the fat from the top of the intense meaty juices in the pitcher; this should leave you with about 1 cup of gingery and garlicky gravy. Check to see whether you need to reheat these juices and if you do, just warm them in a saucepan.

7   Remove the crisp skin and break into pieces, then carve, shred, or pull apart the meat, as wished. Transfer to a warmed dish and pour the meat juices over it, to serve.

APPLE PORK CHOPS
WITH SAUERKRAUT SLAW

Pork, apple, caraway, cabbage: in different permutations, in various countries, these are ingredients that always go well together. Here, this translates into a quick supper with full-on flavor: a juicy pork chop with a zingy slaw. I grew up eating sauerkraut and it rather amuses me now, in the age of the fermentation fad, that it is considered hip. Be that as it may, this apple-and-allspice-glazed chop with its sharp tangle of kraut doesn't need fashionable approbation. But then, nor does any food. It just needs to taste good – which this most emphatically does.

For make ahead/store notes see p.277

1   Put the sauerkraut into a strainer over a bowl and vigorously squeeze out the excess liquid, then leave in the strainer to carry on draining for about 5 minutes.

2   Tip the fully drained sauerkraut into a mixing bowl; unless you want to drink the briny liquid – and some do – that's come out of it, just chuck it away. Add the apple matchsticks, caraway seeds, pepper, cloves, chopped dill, and extra-virgin olive oil. Mix with a fork, and set aside while you cook the pork chops. The acidity of the sauerkraut prevents the apples from discoloring as the slaw stands. I've eaten this the next day, and it still looks bright and fresh.

3   Heat the regular olive oil in a frying pan in which the chops will fit without too much space around them and cook them for 5 minutes each side over a medium-high heat. When you have checked they are cooked through, turn the heat up to high and, using two pairs of tongs – for full comedy value – hold the chops, rind-side down in the pan, for about a minute, so that the fat crisps. Take the pan off the heat while you remove the chops to a couple of waiting plates.

4   Put the pan back on a medium heat and quickly stir in the allspice, followed by the apple juice, and cook for 2 minutes, or until the juice has reduced just a little, to a rich syrup. Don't walk away from the pan. Remove from the heat and sprinkle in the salt. Stir and taste to see if you want any more salt before pouring the glossy gravy over the chops. Serve with the tangy apple sauerkraut slaw.

SERVES 2

Sauerkraut – 2½ cups to give approx. 1 cup when drained and squeezed out
Gala apple – ½, skin left on and cut into matchsticks
Caraway seeds – 1 teaspoon
Pepper – a good grinding
Ground cloves – a pinch
Dill – 1 tablespoon finely chopped
Extra-virgin olive oil – 1 tablespoon
Regular olive oil – 1 tablespoon
Pork chops – 2 (approx. 8 ounces each)
Ground allspice – ¼ teaspoon
Apple juice – ¼ cup
Sea salt flakes or kosher salt – a fat pinch

PORK WITH PRUNES, OLIVES, AND CAPERS

SERVES 4–6

Pork shoulder – 3¼ pounds, diced for a stew

Dry white wine – 1½ cups

Soft dried pitted prunes – 1 heaping cup (approx. 22 prunes)

Pitted black olives – ½ cup

Capers – ½ cup, plus 1 tablespoon of juice from the jar

Dried oregano – ¼ cup

Sea salt flakes or kosher salt – 2½ teaspoons

Pepper – a good grinding

Chicken broth – 1 cup

To serve:
Fresh oregano

This recipe has rather a checkered history. I had been playing about with an old *Joy of Cooking* recipe for Chicken Marbella and, after much tinkering, decided to transfer many of the elements and turn it into a pork stew. It makes sense: pork and prunes are a time-honored combination, after all, and *porc aux pruneaux* was one of my earliest introductions to French home cooking. This is a very different iteration: the molasses sweetness of the prunes is robustly countered by the sharp saltiness of capers – a great many of them, at that – and olives, and bolstered by a generous heap of oregano. What you end up with is a heady, tangy, richly flavored stew, with a gravy that is almost more of a sour-sweet broth.

For all its complexity of flavor, this is so simple to make: the overnight marinade does most of the work for you. It's become one of those recipes I turn to again and again when people are coming over and I want to chuck something in the oven and leave it to do its thing without any input from me.

For make ahead/store notes see p.278

1   Put the pork into a large resealable plastic bag, followed by the wine, prunes, olives, capers and their juice, dried oregano, salt, and pepper. Seal the bag, then put into a shallow dish in the fridge and marinate overnight.

2   Before cooking it, make sure to take the pork out of the fridge in time to get the chill off it; depending on the weather, this should take around 1½ hours. Preheat your oven to 325°F.

3   Tip the pork and marinade into a wide, heavy-based Dutch oven that comes with a lid; the pork will cook more evenly if it is in a relatively shallow layer in the pan. Add the chicken broth, give the pan a stir, then put on the lid and cook in the oven for 2 hours, by which time the pork should be tender.

4   Tear the leaves from a few sprigs of fresh oregano and scatter over the stew before serving.

PORK STEAKS
WITH PORT AND FIGS

For obvious reasons, this is known *chez moi* as pig and fig, and in many ways the combination is a seasonal and wintry version of the Italian summer combo of prosciutto and fresh figs.

It is not advisable to make ahead/store

1   Put the dried figs in a small saucepan, pour over the port and bring to a boil, then turn the heat down a little and let the port bubble cheerfully for 10 minutes until the figs are soft and swollen and the port reduced by about half. Remove from the heat.

2   Mix the flour, spices, and salt together in a resealable plastic bag, drop in the pork steaks, and shake to coat evenly.

3   Over a medium-high heat, warm the oil and butter in a heavy-based frying pan in which the 4 thin chops can fit snugly. Once it starts sizzling, add the pork chops and fry for 2 minutes each side, checking that they are thoroughly cooked through. Transfer the pork chops to a couple of warmed plates while you finish the sauce.

4   Add the figs, port, and a few drops of Worcestershire sauce to the frying pan and, over the heat, stir gently and let it bubble up for 30 seconds or so until rich and syrupy. Remove the pan from the heat.

5   Using tongs, transfer 3 port-bellied figs to each plate, then divide the sauce between the plates, too.

SERVES 2

Soft dried figs – 6
Tawny port – ¾ cup
All-purpose flour – 1 tablespoon
Ground allspice – ½ teaspoon
Ground ginger – 1 teaspoon
Ground cumin – 1 teaspoon
Sea salt flakes or kosher salt – 1 teaspoon
Boneless pork loin chops – 4, thin-cut (approx. 3 ounces each)
Regular olive oil – 1 teaspoon
Unsalted butter – 2 tablespoons
Worcestershire sauce – a few drops

SAUSAGES WITH APPLES AND ONIONS

There is nothing more comfortingly old-fashioned than sausages with apples and onions. This is what my maternal grandmother, who otherwise had an enthusiasm for what my grandfather disparagingly referred to as Landscape Cookery, would give to us when, exhausted by her grandchildren, she hadn't the energy for anything fancier.

I adore the plump whorls of peppery-spiced traditional Cumberland sausages, but this works just as well with twelve good-quality sausages of your choice. And nobody could argue were you to serve the Garlic and Parmesan Mashed Potatoes alongside (see p.66 and halve the quantities). If you're in favor of allium augmentation, then I'd encourage you to make the Cumberland Gravy on p.166 to go with as well.

It is not advisable to make ahead/store

1   Preheat the oven to 400°F. Put the oil, mustard seeds, and thyme into a large, shallow roasting pan, add the onion and apple pieces, sprinkle the salt over, and give everything a good turn to coat well.

2   Push some of the spiced onions and apples aside, to create space for the sausages to sit on the bottom of the pan. Sit the sausages in the spaces allocated, then turn them over so that they're lightly oiled on both sides.

3   Cook in the oven for 50–60 minutes – though start checking at 45 – until the sausages are cooked through and the onions and apples are soft and caramelizing at the edges.

SERVES 4

Regular olive oil – 3 tablespoons
Yellow mustard seeds – 2 teaspoons
Dried thyme – 1 teaspoon
Red onions – 2, peeled, halved, then each half cut into 6 wedges
Gala apples – 4, quartered, cored, then each quarter halved lengthways
Sea salt flakes or kosher salt – 1 teaspoon
12 good quality sausages – (approx. 2 pounds)

FLAT IRON STEAK
WITH A PARSLEY, SHALLOT, AND CAPER SALAD

Flat iron steak is a relatively inexpensive, underused cut of beef, its meat rich and almost gamey, and with a beautiful filigree marbling that keeps it succulent and tender. As with many of these cuts, the key is to marinate slowly and cook quickly. Although it's called a flat iron steak because its shape tapers into a point at the end, I dispense with that bit, asking the butcher instead to cut me 2 chunky steaks (in some circles, apparently, known as patio steaks) from the thick end. It's just much easier to cook evenly this way.

I often use parsley leaves – whole, unchopped – as a salad, and here their robust rasp is admirably matched by the fierceness of the shallot and sting of the capers.

While I would never condone eating steak without English mustard, I am all for an extra sunburst dollop of the Golden Garlic Mayonnaise, see p.115, on the side as well.

For make ahead/store notes see p.278

SERVES 4

**Flat iron steaks cut from the
thick end** – 2 (9–10 ounces each)

For the marinade:
Vegetable oil – ¼ cup
Worcestershire sauce –
2 tablespoons
Soy sauce – 2 tablespoons
**Raw unfiltered apple cider
vinegar** – 1 tablespoon

For the salad:
Shallot – 1 large, peeled and cut into
fine half-moons
Capers – 2 tablespoons, plus
2 tablespoons of juice from the jar
Italian parsley – leaves from a
large bunch, to give 4 cups loosely
packed
Extra-virgin olive oil – 1 teaspoon

1   Put the steaks into a resealable plastic bag with all the marinade
    ingredients, seal well, and leave on a flat plate or dish in the fridge
    overnight.

2   Take the steaks out of the fridge about an hour before you want to
    cook them and leave, still in the marinade, to reach room temperature.

3   While you wait, put the half-moons of shallot into a small bowl and
    pour the caper juice over. Fork to mix, then tamp down a little and
    leave to steep.

4   Heat a grill pan or heavy-based frying pan until it is very hot, then
    take the steaks out of the marinade, shaking any liquid that clings
    to them back into the bag.

5   I find that this cut takes a little longer to cook than other steaks,
    and it seems to puff up as it does so. For rare (which is how this is
    best eaten, as it will get tough otherwise) give the steaks – if they're
    around ¾ inch thick – 5 minutes each side; if you have thinner steaks
    they'll obviously need less time. The remnants of marinade on the
    surface of the steaks will scorch flavorsomely, though turn the heat
    down if you think they're burning.

6   Once the steaks have had their time, lift them out onto a piece of
    aluminum foil and wrap them loosely to form a baggy – but tightly
    sealed – parcel. Leave to rest for 5 minutes.

7   Put the capers and parsley leaves in a large bowl, then scrape in the
    sliced shallot, and any juice, and toss well. Add the teaspoon of extra-
    virgin olive oil and toss patiently again, then transfer to a shallow
    salad bowl or plate.

8   Unwrap the steaks carefully; you don't want to lose any juice (though
    there won't be a lot) that may have collected in the parcel. Transfer
    the steaks to a board and cut, diagonally and across the grain, into
    slices. Leave on the board or transfer to a warmed plate, pour the
    juices from the foil over them, and serve with the salad.

ROAST TOP ROUND
WITH CARAMELIZED ONIONS

Marinating the beef overnight makes the meat – which, lamentably, can so often be slightly tough – wonderfully juicy. Of course, it's also important not to overcook it. Much as I resist the professional cooking approach, I do love a kitchen gadget. And I have come reluctantly to accept that a probe thermometer is the best way to make sure meat's cooked just how you want it. For rare, the probe should read 125°F and for medium, 140°F; for well done, you're on your own.

I tend to make the caramelized onions (which in the '90s used to be called Onion Marmalade) while the beef's marinating. You don't have to follow suit, but I like them cold, though most definitely not chilled. If you, too, wish to cook them in advance, take them out of the fridge at the same time as the marinated beef, letting both come to room temperature at the same time. This is in every way perfect with the Tomato and Horseradish Salad on p.89.

For make ahead/store notes see p.278

1 Put the beef and all the marinade ingredients into a large resealable plastic bag, seal, give it a good squelch, and turn the beef in the marinade quite a bit, before putting it on a dish in the fridge overnight.

2 When you want to make the caramelized onions (whether while the beef is marinating, or when it's coming to room temperature before it goes in the oven), heat the oil in a wide, heavy-based saucepan, add the sliced onions, sprinkling with the salt, and cook over a medium-high heat for about 7 minutes until softened, turning them often so that they cook evenly and don't scorch.

3 Stir in the sugar, turn the heat to very low, and let them carry on cooking, turning them in the pan every now and again, for about 45 minutes, or until they have become thick and sticky. Keep checking them to make sure they're not burning and, if you feel they are, add a splash of water to the pan.

4 Take off the heat and stir in the tangy pomegranate molasses. If you're making these in advance, decant into a bowl to cool. Otherwise, just leave in the pan until you serve.

SERVES 4 WITH – FOR ME, ESSENTIAL – GENEROUS LEFTOVERS

For the beef and marinade:
Beef top round – 2¼ pounds
Regular olive oil – ½ cup
Sea salt flakes or kosher salt – 2 teaspoons, plus more for sprinkling
Thyme – 6 sprigs, plus more for sprinkling
Garlic – 4 fat cloves, bruised and slightly splintered with the flat side of a wide-bladed knife, then slipped out of their skins
Crushed red pepper flakes – ½ teaspoon
Lemon – 1, finely grated zest and juice

For the caramelized onions:
Regular olive oil – 2 tablespoons
Red onions – 4 (approx. 1½ pounds), peeled and thinly sliced
Sea salt flakes or kosher salt – 1 teaspoon
Light brown sugar – 1 tablespoon
Pomegranate molasses – 1 tablespoon

5   About 1½ hours before you want to roast the beef, remove it from the fridge to get to room temperature, at which time preheat the oven to 425°F.

6   Remove the beef from its marinade and transfer to a small, shallow roasting pan, with a good sprinkle of salt. For beef that's juicily rare in the middle and medium rare at either end, roast in the hot oven for about 45 minutes, though this is where some probe-work might be advisable (see recipe introduction). Or you can slip in the point of a sharp knife and take a peek at the meat to check. Once it's ready, take it out of the oven, tent with aluminum foil, and let it rest for 10–15 minutes. Transfer the beef to a board, carve thinly, and arrange on a warmed serving plate, then pour the scant juices which have collected in the pan over it. Sprinkle lightly with salt and strew with a few sprigs of thyme. Serve with the caramelized onions.

SIRLOIN STEAKS
WITH ANCHOVY CREAM SAUCE

SERVES 2

Sirloin steaks – 2 (approx. 8 ounces each)

Sea salt flakes or kosher salt – 1 teaspoon

Regular olive oil – 2 teaspoons

Unsalted butter – 1 teaspoon, soft

Anchovy fillets – 4, finely chopped

Garlic – 1 fat clove, peeled and minced

Chives – 2 tablespoons finely chopped

Heavy cream – 5 tablespoons

There is something about an old-fashioned steak in cream sauce that I just can't resist. This particular version is, in a manner of speaking, a saline take on a classic *steak au poivre*. Instead of giving the cream a punch of pepper, I bring the sea-water saltiness of anchovies into play, melting them into the cream once the steaks are cooked, to make a deeply flavored, pale buff sauce, flecked with chives.

It is not advisable to make ahead/store

1   Take the steaks out of the fridge, put them on a plate or board, and sprinkle them with half the salt – about ¼ teaspoon on each steak – then turn them over, and do the same on the other side. Leave them to come to room temperature. Tear off two pieces of aluminum foil, large enough to wrap the steaks loosely later.

2   Pour the oil into a heavy-based frying pan in which the steaks will fit without too much empty space around them, and turn the heat on high. When the oil is hot, add the steaks. I like meat rare and so, with steaks around ¾ inch thick, I give them 3 minutes each side, though do keep an eye on the pan – it wants to be hot enough to sear the outside, but not to burn it. To tell if the steaks are cooked as you want them, just press them a little: if they feel very bouncy, they're rare; if you meet with just a little resistance, they're medium; well done steaks have no give at all. And, if you're unsure, you can just cut into one with the point of a sharp knife.

3   Take the pan off the heat, remove the steaks to their waiting pieces of foil, and wrap each one into a baggy, but tightly sealed parcel.

4   Put the pan back, now over a low heat, add the butter, and when it's all but melted, stir in the chopped anchovies, followed by the minced garlic, and cook, stirring for a minute or so, letting the anchovies seem, themselves, to melt into the butter. Add most of the chives, then pour in the cream, letting it bubble up and thicken slightly as you stir. Remove immediately from the heat.

5   Unwrap the steaks and transfer them to a couple of warmed plates, pouring any juices that have collected into the pan and stirring them into the cream. Pour this sauce over the steaks and sprinkle with the remaining chives.

QUEEN OF PUDDINGS

I wasn't brought up on nursery food, so this sort of old-fashioned British pudding holds a certain exotic charm for me. Traditionally, a Queen of Puddings is made with bread crumbs, but this is the Marie Antoinette version, using brioche instead.

Of course, in the normal run of things, I don't have stale brioche lying about, but you can quite easily stale it by leaving the slices on a wire rack for a good few hours or overnight. If time is pressing, put the slices on a wire rack sitting in a roasting pan, and heat in an oven preheated to 220°F for 10–15 minutes. I tend to stale and crumb a whole brioche loaf at a time, so that I have the wherewithal to make this quickly whenever I want. Divide the crumbs into portions of 2½ cups, which is how much you need per pudding. I then freeze the crumbs, measured out ready, in tightly sealed bags in eager readiness to make this.

For make ahead/store notes see p.278

1 Process the stale brioche into crumbs and tip into a mixing bowl.

2 Grease your pie dish with butter and preheat the oven to 325°F.

3 Warm the milk in a saucepan along with the butter, lemon zest, vanilla extract, sugar, and a pinch of salt, just until the butter's melted.

4 Whisk the yolks in a large bowl or pitcher, pour the warm milk mixture on top, and whisk to combine, then pour this over the crumbs in their bowl and leave for 10 minutes, before transferring to the greased dish. Bake for 20 minutes, or until the top is just set, although the crumb-custard will still be wibbly underneath.

5 Take the dish out of the oven; the custardy brioche will firm up a little on the surface while it stands, waiting.

6 In a small bowl, whisk the 2 teaspoons of lemon juice into the preserves: you want a soft, pourable consistency. If the preserves are too thick, simply warm in a small saucepan. Set aside while you get on with the topping.

SERVES 6–8

For the base:
Brioche – 6 ounces, cut into slices and left to stale (see recipe introduction), to give 2½ cups crumbs
Unsalted butter – 3 tablespoons, soft, plus more for greasing
Whole milk – 2 cups
Lemon – 1, finely grated zest, plus 2 teaspoons of juice
Vanilla extract – 1 teaspoon
Sugar – 3 tablespoons
Fine sea salt – a pinch
Eggs – 4 large, yolks only (reserve whites for meringue topping)
Plum (or other) preserves – ¾ cup

For the topping:
Egg whites – 4 large (from eggs above)
Superfine sugar – ½ cup, plus more for sprinkling

1 x 6-cup oval pie dish, approx. 11 x 8 x 2 inches

7   Whisk the egg whites in a grease-free bowl until they form firm peaks, then gradually whisk in the superfine sugar, until you have a thick and shiny meringue.

8   Pour the lemon-spritzed preserves over the crumb-custard, smoothing it – with the lightest touch – over the top. Cover the preserves-topped custard with the meringue, making sure it comes right to the edges to seal it well. Use a fork to pull the gleaming meringue topping into little peaks, and sprinkle with ½ teaspoon or so of superfine sugar.

9   Put the dish back in the oven and bake for about 20 minutes until the meringue is bronzed and crisp on top. Let it stand out of the oven for about 15 minutes before serving.

APPLE GINGERJACK

Grasmere Gingerbread, a specialty from the Lake District in England, was the original inspiration for this recipe, although I can't say that it would be noticeable to anyone in Grasmere. There is something of its ginger-hot sandiness, but really the topping over the sharp apples is more like a soft oat bar, called a flapjack in the UK and hence its jaunty name.

It's not to be eaten piping hot, but warm or even just hovering above room temperature. This makes life very much easier, as you can cook it and get it out of the oven before you sit down for dinner. Actually, I find it all too easy to eat it cold, which makes leftovers a real boon.

If you can't get the stone-ground oatmeal, you can approximate it by blitzing 2 cups quick cooking oats in the processor until the flakes have all but turned into sand; whatever you do don't buy oatbran by mistake.

For make ahead/store notes see p.278

1   Preheat the oven to 400°F and get out your pie dish.

2   Gently melt the butter in a heavy-based saucepan in which the apples will fit, if not in a single layer, then not too heaped up on each other; I use a pan of about 9 inches diameter if that helps. Once the butter's melted, stir in the syrup then tumble in the apples, and cook over a medium heat for 15 minutes or so, stirring frequently, until the apples start softening. Transfer to the pie dish and use a silicone spatula (it does the job best) to scrape every bit of buttery, syrupy, appley juices into the dish.

3   Mix the oatmeal, light brown sugar, 4 teaspoons of ginger, and the baking soda together, using your fingers to break up any lumps in the sugar. Set aside for a moment.

4   In the same scraped-out pan, heat the milk and butter gently, until the butter's melted and the milk has been brought up to boiling point. Take the pan off the heat. Add the oatmeal mixture and stir, beating a little with a wooden spoon or flat whisk, until smooth; it will thicken as you do so. Swiftly pour and scrape over the apples, then spread it out to make sure it covers them, and goes right to the edges of the dish.

SERVES 6–8

For the base:
Unsalted butter – 1 tablespoon
Light corn syrup – 2 tablespoons
Granny Smith apples – 1¾ pounds (approx. 6), peeled, cored, and cut into approx. 1 inch chunks

For the topping:
Stone-ground oatmeal (gluten-free if required) – 1½ cups
Light brown sugar – ⅓ cup
Ground ginger – 4 teaspoons, plus ¼ teaspoon for sprinkling
Baking soda – ½ teaspoon
Whole milk – 1 cup
Unsalted butter – 1 stick (8 tablespoons), soft, cut into cubes

To sprinkle over:
Turbinado sugar – 1½ tablespoons

To serve:
Heavy cream or crème anglaise

1 x 9-inch pie dish

5   Mix the ¼ teaspoon of ground ginger with the turbinado sugar and sprinkle on top. Transfer to the oven and bake for about 30 minutes until the apples are soft and the top has firmly set underneath its beautiful golden brown, sugar-sprinkled crust. Let it stand out of the oven for at least 30 minutes, as it is best warm – even at room temperature – rather than hot. In fact, I prefer to let it stand out of the oven for about an hour before bringing it to the table. Serve with heavy cream or, for extra coziness, crème anglaise.

WHITE CHOCOLATE CHEESECAKE

The shades of my ancestors are, no doubt, horrified that 1) this is an unbaked cheesecake and 2) white chocolate finds its way into it. So be it.

Besides, I have no need to be defensive about this: the white chocolate is only a delicate presence here; nothing to offend a white-chocolate-hater. And, moreover, it helps the cheesecake set in the fridge overnight to a perfect, tenderly firm consistency.

While I love this pale, plain and unadorned, it can be beautifully partyfied by a sprinkling of chopped pistachios and a jewel-bright scattering of pomegranate seeds.

For make ahead/store notes see p.278

1   Put the pieces of white chocolate into a heatproof bowl that will sit on top of a saucepan. Fill the pan with a small amount of water, just enough to come up about 1½ inches up the sides, and bring to a boil. Sit the bowl of chocolate on top, making sure the base of the bowl doesn't touch the water. Turn the heat down and let the white chocolate melt very gently, every now and then giving it a careful stir with a silicone spatula. Once there are only a few small lumps of unmelted chocolate left, give it another stir then remove the bowl and sit it somewhere for about 10 minutes, until the chocolate remains liquid but is cooled to room temperature.

2   For the base, break the cookies into a food processor and blitz until you have almost all crumbs. Add the butter and process again until the mixture starts to clump and cleave to the blade. If doing this by hand, put the cookies into a bag, crush to crumbs, then melt the butter and stir into the cookie crumbs until well mixed.

3   Press the crumb mixture into the springform cake pan, letting some come a little way up the sides. The back of a soup or serving spoon is the easiest tool for the already easy job here. Stash the pan in the fridge while you get on with the cheesecake filling.

4   Beat the cream cheese in a bowl that will take all the ingredients later – a wooden spoon is fine here – until it is soft. Gently fold in the slightly cooled, melted white chocolate.

5   Softly whip the cream so it is thickened but the peaks don't hold their shape, then fold it into the white chocolate mixture in two

For the filling:
Good quality white chocolate – 7 ounces, roughly chopped
Cream cheese – 10 ounces (1¼ cups), at room temperature, drained of any liquid
Heavy cream – 1¼ cups
Lemon – 1 teaspoon of juice
Vanilla extract – 1 teaspoon

For the base:
Gingersnap cookies – 6 ounces, crumbled, to give 1¼ cups loosely packed
Unsalted butter – 3 tablespoons, soft

1 x 8-inch springform cake pan

batches. Add the lemon juice and vanilla extract and fold these in, then pour and scrape the pale, almost-moussy mixture into the crumb-lined pan. Smooth the top, cover the pan with plastic wrap, and refrigerate overnight before serving.

6   When you're ready to eat it, make sure it's been out of the fridge for 10 minutes before unclipping from the pan and cutting it into slices. Don't expect to be able to remove the whole cheesecake from the pan's base unless you are both patient and dexterous. I was once foolhardy enough to try…

ROSE AND PEPPER PAVLOVA
WITH STRAWBERRIES AND PASSIONFRUIT

The flavors sound so bold here and yet taste so delicate. My maternal grandfather used to eat strawberries with a grinding of black pepper; he insisted it made their berried freshness sing. I prefer to add it to the pavlova base, pairing its perfumed warmth with some rosewater, giving the marshmallow-bellied meringue the huskiest hint of Turkish delight. Macerating the strawberries in passionfruit juice both heightens their flavor and brings its own sour-sweet fragrance.

It is best to make the pavlova base a good few hours, if not a day ahead, then store it in an airtight container. Certainly, it must be completely cold before being topped with cream and fruit.

For make ahead/store notes see p.278

SERVES 8–12

For the base:
Eggs – 6 large, at room temperature, whites only
Superfine sugar – 1¾ cups plus 2 tablespoons
Cornstarch – 2½ teaspoons
Ready-ground black pepper – ¼ teaspoon
White wine vinegar – 2 teaspoons
Rosewater – ½ teaspoon

For the topping:
Strawberries – 10 ounces
Passionfruit – 3
Sugar – 2 teaspoons
Heavy cream – 1¼ cups

1   Preheat the oven to 350°F and line a baking sheet with parchment paper.

2   In a grease-free bowl, whisk the egg whites until firm peaks form, and then beat in the superfine sugar a spoonful at a time until the meringue is stiff and shiny. Be patient: it takes a little time to thicken glossily.

3   Sprinkle the cornstarch, pepper, vinegar, and rosewater over the meringue, then, by hand, gently fold everything until it is thoroughly mixed in. Mound onto the lined baking sheet in a fat disc approximately 9 inches in diameter, smoothing the sides and top. Place in the oven, then immediately turn the temperature down to 300°F and bake for 1 hour.

4   Take out of the oven and leave to cool, but do not leave anywhere cold as this will make it crack too dramatically. You'll always get some cracks though, so don't fret. If you think your kitchen is too cold, then drape the pavlova base loosely with a clean tea towel.

5   When the meringue is cold and you're ready to eat, turn the pavlova base onto a large flat plate with the underside uppermost.

6   Hull each strawberry and cut, from hulled end to the tip, to make 3 slices, putting them into a shallow bowl as you go. Cut the passionfruit into halves then, using a small strainer over a pitcher or bowl, spoon the juice and seeds into the strainer, pressing all the juice out into the pitcher. Discard the seeds, then pour the juice

over the strawberries and sprinkle with the sugar, leaving them to macerate while you get on with the cream.

7   Whip the cream until thick and airy but still soft, and spread on top of the pavlova base in a swirly-mound, working all the way to the edges so that it is evenly covered.

8   Spoon the shiny strawberries in their juice over the top – the swirls of cream will catch some of the golden yellow of the passionfruit – and bear proudly aloft to the table.

CHOCOLATE OLIVE OIL MOUSSE

I first came across a version of this voluptuously soft, rich chocolate mousse at Morito, one of my favorite places to eat in London. Then – as these things tend to happen – I started finding it everywhere. The olive oil doesn't just bring its resonant flavor to the mousse, it creates its smooth, soft texture. Go for a smooth but still spicy rather than raspingly peppery extra-virgin olive oil, and use the absolute best quality you can.

For make ahead/store notes see p.278

1   Melt the chocolate either in the microwave or in a large heatproof bowl suspended over a saucepan of simmering water (but not touching the water), making sure – either way – you remove it from the heat before it is completely melted, then stir it gently so that the last little pieces of chocolate dissolve. Leave to cool for 10 minutes. Stir in the oil to combine and set aside for a moment.

2   Whisk the egg whites and a pinch of sea salt flakes in a grease-free bowl until you have firm peaks. Set aside for the moment.

3   In another bowl, large enough to take everything later, whisk the yolks, sugar, and ¼ teaspoon of sea salt flakes until pale, thick, and about doubled in volume. You don't need to clean the beaters when going from whites to yolks.

4   Gradually pour the chocolate-oil mixture into the beaten yolks and fold to mix completely. Add a third of the beaten egg whites and fold in vigorously to lighten the mixture; no need to be delicate at this stage. Now gently fold in another third of the egg whites and, when that second lot is incorporated, fold in the final third leaving behind any liquid at the bottom of the bowl of whites. No white streaks should be visible.

5   In a rather freeform way, gently spoon the mousse into your ramekins or cups. To get the right texture – soft and satiny, rather than set like a more traditional mousse – you can either refrigerate for 20 minutes then eat straight away, or for exactly one hour and then take out to come to room temperature for 40 minutes before eating.

SERVES 6

Bittersweet chocolate, preferably min. 70% cocoa solids – 6 ounces, roughly chopped
Extra-virgin olive oil – 7 tablespoons
Eggs – 4 large, at room temperature, separated
Sea salt flakes – a pinch, plus ¼ teaspoon—or halve amounts if using fine sea salt
Superfine sugar – ¼ cup

6 x ½ cup ramekins or 8 espresso cups

GINGER WINE SYLLABUB

There is nothing quite like the celestially airy, cloud-like kiss of a syllabub.

It is not advisable to make ahead/store.

1   Pour the ginger wine and lemon juice into a bowl or pitcher.

2   Starting off with the coarsely-grated ginger on a plate or board near the mixing bowl, take a piece of paper towel, add 1 tablespoon of the grated ginger in the center and, moving swiftly, pull up the sides to form a little swag bag and squeeze on it, wringing the ginger juice out into the bowl or pitcher. With a fresh piece of paper towel, do the same with the second tablespoon. These 2 tablespoons of grated ginger should yield about 2 teaspoons of ginger juice. Add the sugar and stir until dissolved.

3   Put the cream into the bowl of a freestanding mixer or a large mixing bowl. Whisk until the cream just starts to hold its shape, then whisk in the ginger wine mixture until you have a soft, bulky cloud mixture. It should be thick, but airily so: when you lift the whisk out of the cream, the peak it makes should only just hold its shape.

4   Dollop gently into your glasses, giving each a soft-serve peak at the top, and put in the fridge for 30 minutes to an hour; any longer and they will lose their defining lightness.

SERVES 4–6

Ginger wine (such as Stone's) – ⅔ cup
Lemon – 2 tablespoons of juice
Fresh ginger – 2 tablespoons coarsely grated
Confectioners' sugar – ¼ cup
Heavy cream – 1⅓ cups

To serve:
Shortbread cookies, brandy snaps, or any other cookies of your choice

4 x large or 6 x small wine glasses

WARM BLONDIE PUDDING CAKE

When I was a judge on MasterChef Australia in 2016, Chloe Bowles, one of the contestants, came up with a batch of quite magnificent gluten-free blondies, and very kindly gave me the recipe; I wasn't going to leave the country without it. I have taken great liberties with it and in the process turned it into a warm, squidgy dessert, to be eaten with a tangy splodge of crème fraîche and a tumble of sharp raspberries. Insistently sweet, it does need the counterbalance.

You can, of course, eat them as blondies, in traditional fashion, in which case I'd give them another 5 minutes in the oven, loosely covered with aluminum foil. Let them get completely cold, then put in the fridge to chill completely before cutting them into squares.

For make ahead/store notes see p.278

1   Preheat the oven to 325°F and very lightly grease your dish.

2   Melt the butter and chocolate in a heavy-based saucepan very, very gently. Keep the heat really low and be patient. Don't stir, just lift the pan up and give it a swirl every now and then.

3   Once it is a sludgy paste in buttery liquid – how charmingly attractive that sounds – remove from the heat before adding the sugar and ginger, and stir gently to combine. It should amalgamate into a glossy-looking fudge. Allow to cool off the stove for 10 minutes. Don't worry if the butter and chocolate separate as it stands: all will come good when you add the eggs.

4   Stir in the eggs and keep stirring until they're completely incorporated. Add the chopped walnuts and almond flour and, again, stir gently to combine.

5   Pour into your prepared dish and bake in the oven for 35–40 minutes, or until golden brown on top, crisp at the edges, and beginning to come away from the sides of the dish. It should feel a little squidgy under its just-firm top; a cake tester will not come out completely clean, but with a few damp crumbs clinging to it.

6   Leave to cool for 30–40 minutes before cutting into it, and serve with crème fraîche and raspberries.

MAKES 9 LARGE SQUARES

Unsalted butter – 1 stick plus 5 tablespoons (13 tablespoons), soft, cut into cubes or spooned into blobs, plus more for greasing

Good-quality white chocolate – 3 ounces, chopped into smallish pieces

Light brown sugar – ¾ cup plus 2 tablespoons

Ground ginger – 2 teaspoons

Eggs – 3 large, at room temperature, lightly whisked

Walnut pieces – 1 cup, roughly chopped so that you have both small pieces and dusty rubble

Fine almond flour – 1½ cups

To serve:
Crème fraîche
Raspberries

1 x approx. 9-inch square baking dish

STICKY TOFFEE PUDDING

The Lake District has given us many great things: some of the most beautiful scenery in the British Isles, William Wordsworth, Grasmere Gingerbread, and the glory that is Sticky Toffee Pudding.

My STP is altogether deeper and darker than the original version: it is still sweet, but the dark brown sugar and molasses give it an almost savage intensity. It seems redolent of ginger, cloves, allspice – and yet none of these spices are used. It's a miracle. I don't understand it – but then, miracles are not to be questioned.

It shouldn't be eaten piping hot, but warm; once the sponge has been topped with a glaze of the sauce, and had its 30 minutes' waiting time, it will be at optimum temperature. And cold – should you have any leftovers – a slab of it cut from the dish tastes like the most magnificent sticky gingerbread.

You will find it easier to measure out the molasses if you run your spoon under a hot tap first.

For make ahead/store notes see p.278

1   Preheat the oven to 350°F and lightly grease your dish. Put the chopped dates, boiling water, and baking soda into a bowl, give a stir, and then leave for 10 minutes.

2   Cream the butter and molasses until well mixed, then add the sugar and mix again, beating out any lumps. Beat in an egg and keep beating – scraping down as necessary – until completely incorporated, then do likewise with the other egg. Beating more gently, add the flour and baking powder until you have a smooth, thick batter.

3   Using a fork, stir the soaked dates, squishing them a bit, then pour the dates and their liquid into the batter and beat gently to mix in.

4   Pour and scrape into your prepared dish and bake in the oven for 30–35 minutes, or until a cake tester comes out clean.

5   While the sponge is in the oven, you can make the sauce. Melt the butter, sugar, and molasses over a very low heat in a heavy-based saucepan. Once the butter's melted, stir gently until everything else is melted too. Now stir in the cream, then turn up the heat and when it's bubbling and hot, take it off the heat.

CUTS INTO 9 GENEROUS SLABS

For the sponge:
Soft dried pitted dates – 7 ounces (approx. 15 large dates), roughly chopped
Water from a freshly boiled kettle – ¾ cup plus 1 tablespoon
Baking soda – 1 teaspoon
Unsalted butter – 5 tablespoons, soft, plus more for greasing
Molasses – 2 tablespoons
Dark brown sugar – ¼ cup
Eggs – 2 large, at room temperature
All-purpose flour – 1 cup plus 2 tablespoons
Baking powder – 2 teaspoons

For the sauce:
Unsalted butter – 1¼ sticks (10 tablespoons), soft
Dark brown sugar – 1½ cups
Molasses – 1 tablespoon
Heavy cream – ¾ cup plus 1 tablespoon, plus more to serve

1 x approx. 9-inch square baking dish

6   As soon as it's out of the oven, prick the cooked sponge all over with a toothpick and pour about a quarter of the warm sauce over, easing it to the edges with a spatula so that the sponge is entirely topped with a thick sticky glaze. Put a lid on the remaining sauce in the pan to keep it warm.

7   Leave for 20–30 minutes, or up to 1 hour is fine, then take to the table, with the rest of the sauce in a pitcher, and cream to serve.

MAPLE ROASTED PLUMS
WITH CINNAMON BROWN SUGAR YOGURT

Plain whole milk Greek yogurt – ¾ cup

Dark brown sugar – 2 tablespoons

Ground cinnamon – 1 teaspoon

Unsalted butter – 2 tablespoons, soft

Maple syrup – ¼ cup

Star anise – 4

Slightly under-ripe red plums – 8, halved and pits removed

This makes excellent use of fruit bought in hopefulness, but whose flesh proves too disappointingly unyielding to bite into juicily. Lusciously ripe plums would just dissolve into a pulpy fuzz in the heat of the oven. Nor do you want them as hard as billiard balls: for one thing, it makes removing the pits either painful or impossible. Caught in the middle, the plums keep their rhubarb sharpness as they cook and soften in the smoky, subdued sweetness of the maple syrup.

For make ahead/store notes see p.278

1   Preheat the oven to 350°F. Stir the yogurt, sugar, and cinnamon together well in a bowl, then leave to stand to let the sugar dissolve and the flavors deepen.

2   In an ovenproof dish, in which the halved plums will fit snugly, warm the butter, maple syrup, and star anise just until the butter has melted; you can do this on the stove or in the oven depending on what you're using. Either way, remove the dish from the heat.

3   Place the plums in the dish, cut-side down, then turn them straightaway cut-side up, transfer to the oven, and bake for 20 minutes, at which time you should baste the plums with the syrupy juices, now a gash-gold-vermillion. Then give them another 10–20 minutes until they are just soft – a quick prod with a small fork should let you know – but still holding their shape. Let the dish sit out of the oven for 10 minutes before serving, with the aromatic yogurt in a bowl alongside.

BUTTERSCOTCH POTS

When I was a child, my idea of a treat beyond measure was butterscotch-flavored Angel Delight, a chemical-tasting mousse in a package, made by whisking milk into its tipped-out contents of flour, flavorings, and God knows what else; my fondly remembered love of which says more about the romance of nostalgia than it does about the dessert itself. Still, inspiration comes in many forms, and this one has created a silky, richly smooth caramel pudding, with something childishly comforting about it.

For make ahead/store notes see p.278

SERVES 2

Cornstarch – 4 teaspoons
Whole milk – ¾ cup
Egg – 1 large, yolk only
Fine sea salt – ¼ teaspoon
Unsalted butter – 1 tablespoon, soft
Sugar – ¼ cup
Heavy cream – 7 tablespoons

**2 x approx. ⅔ cup ramekins
or heatproof glasses**

1 Put the cornstarch into a bowl, then slowly whisk in the milk and keep whisking until you have banished every lump. Now beat in the egg yolk and salt, and set aside somewhere within easy reach of the stove.

2 Melt the butter in a small, heavy-based saucepan, over a medium-high heat, and then whisk in the sugar. It will look grainy and clumpy at these early stages – rather like lemon sorbet – but keep whisking and it will become first a toffee-like goo, and then a smooth and placid butterscotch-colored lake. Once it begins to bubble, swirl the pan frequently, until it becomes a rich, deep, glossy teak, and begins to smoke. Don't let it burn, obviously, but don't be so timorous that you fail to get that smoky caramel taste.

3 Take the pan off the heat and whisk in the cream, which will bubble up vociferously, so be careful, and keep whisking until it stops bubbling. Should there be any lumps at this stage, simply return the pan to a low heat and stir until dissolved.

4 Pour half this hot mixture into the milk and egg and whisk to incorporate. When it's smooth, pour the contents of the bowl back into the caramel pan, using a spatula to scrape every last bit in, put over a medium-high heat and whisk until it is gorgeously thick. This should take a minute or so.

5 For ease, pour into a heatproof pitcher and thence into your serving glasses. The minute you've filled the glasses, press some plastic wrap or dampened parchment paper directly on top of the butterscotch puddings to prevent a skin forming and leave to cool. You can eat these as soon as they're cold. On serving, remove the plastic wrap or parchment paper and swirl the tops with the back of a teaspoon. Should you feel like spooning whipped cream on top and grating some chocolate over it, why should I be the person to stop you?

PASSIONFRUIT ICE-CREAM CAKE
WITH COCONUT-CARAMEL SAUCE

A dream to eat, and a doddle to make.

Ever since my first pavlova, I've been utterly sold on the combination – smooth, chewy, sour-sweet, and fragrant – of cream, meringue, and passionfruit. And to turn these ingredients into a coolly elegant ice-cream cake, you need do nothing more than stir them all together and leave to set in the freezer overnight: a no-cook, no-churn, no-stress affair.

For make ahead/store notes see p.278

1   Line your loaf pan with plastic wrap, leaving plenty of overhang on the sides of the pan so that you can cover the top later.

2   Whip the heavy cream until ripples start to appear in the bowl and it's slightly thickened but not stiff.

3   Add the pulp, seeds, and juice of the passionfruit, then the Cointreau (or other liqueur) and fold briefly just to combine. Go gently.

4   Using your hands, break up the meringue cookies, making a mixture of both dust and small pieces of meringue, and very gently fold in, until evenly mixed; along with the alcohol, it's the fine dispersal of meringue that keeps the ice cream smooth as it freezes.

5   Spoon gently into the lined loaf pan, pressing down as you go so that you don't have any gaps or air pockets. Once the mixture is carefully packed in and the top smoothed, cover with the plastic wrap overhang, then wrap the pan in another sheet of plastic wrap before putting into the freezer overnight.

6   The sauce is to be served cold, so you can get on with it now; I find it makes life very much easier if you can make everything ahead. Gently melt the butter, sugars, and syrup in a deep, heavy-based saucepan of about 8 inches diameter and, once melted, turn the heat up a little and let it simmer – bubbling up a bit – for 3 minutes. Lift the pan up off the heat every now and again and give it a swirl.

7   With the pan off the stove momentarily, add the coconut cream and swirl again, then put back on the heat and cook at a fast simmer for about 10 minutes, stirring every now and then, until it's the color of peanut butter and slightly thickened (it will get properly thick

ICE-CREAM CAKE:
CUTS INTO 8 SLICES

SAUCE: MAKES APPROX.
¾ CUP

For the ice-cream cake:
Heavy cream – 1¼ cups
Passionfruit – 4
**Cointreau, Grand Marnier
or Triple Sec** – 4 teaspoons
Meringue cookies – 4 ounces

For the sauce:
Unsalted butter – 3 tablespoons
Light brown sugar – ¼ cup
Sugar – ¼ cup
Light corn syrup – 3 tablespoons
**Unsweetened coconut cream (not
creamed coconut)** – 1 cup

**1 x 1-pound loaf pan, approx.
7½ x 5 x 3 inches**

once it's cooled). It does bubble and spurt a little as it cooks, rather like those municipal water features – the dancing fountains – that children love running through.

8   Pour it into a heatproof pitcher and leave to cool to room temperature. The sauce will thicken too much if refrigerated, so if it has been in the fridge, remember to take it out in time for it to lose its chill.

9   When you are ready to serve the ice-cream cake, take the pan out of the deep-freeze, remove the outer layer of plastic wrap, then lift out the ice-cream cake and sit it on a board before fully unwrapping. Cut into thick slices; if you don't want to eat all the cake at one sitting, wrap the remaining unsliced loaf up well and put it back in the freezer.

10 Put a slice onto each plate and then leave to soften a little, for 5–10 minutes, depending on the warmth of your kitchen.

11 Zigzag some of the coconut-caramel sauce over each slice – stirring it briskly first if it's got too thick – and pour the rest into a small pitcher to take to the table alongside.

NO-CHURN CHOCOLATE TRUFFLE ICE CREAM

MAKES APPROX. 1½ PINTS

Heavy cream – 1¼ cups

Unsweetened cocoa powder – 3 tablespoons, sifted if lumpy

Instant espresso powder – 1 teaspoon

Condensed milk – ½ x 14-ounce can (⅔ cup)

Dark rum – 3 tablespoons

2 x 1 pint airtight containers

This tastes exactly as its title suggests: a rich, dark, bitter, boozy rum truffle in ice cream form.

Don't be alarmed if the mixture seems to seize as you whisk it; while you may initially be faced with a thick, quite dry mixture, the alcohol makes sure that it ends up smooth and soft once it has been frozen. For this reason, the rum cannot be left out, as the Bourbon can in the Salted Caramel Ice Cream on p.230.

For make ahead/store notes see p.278

1   Pour the heavy cream into the bowl of a freestanding mixer or, if you're using an electric hand whisk, just in a large bowl. Sprinkle the cocoa on top, followed by the instant espresso powder, and fold into the cream; expect the cocoa to sit mostly on top of the cream and cling to the sides of the bowl at this stage.

2   Whisk the contents of the bowl until it all starts to thicken. Once the mixture has formed soft peaks, add the condensed milk, and drizzle in the rum very slowly, beating all the time until thick. Then give a good fold by hand with a silicone spatula.

3   Fill your airtight containers (the second one will be only half to three-quarters full) and freeze for 8 hours or overnight. Serve straight from the freezer.

NO-CHURN BOURBON SALTED CARAMEL ICE CREAM

Salted caramel may no longer be the *dernier cri* in modish eating, but this doesn't trouble me and it shouldn't trouble you either. I can never get enough of the stuff. Food is either good, or it isn't, and to cloud this with anxious fretting about whether it is hip enough — no doubt a pressing issue for fashionable restaurants — is, at its most charitable, just silly. Quite frankly, they've been making *caramel au beurre salé* in Brittany for generations, without any regard for the frivolous ebb and flow of fads.

I've given a range of measurements for both salt and Bourbon, but go slowly, tasting as you add, and stop when it feels right for you; bear in mind that flavors are less pronounced when the mixture is frozen. And much as I love the deep-throated warmth of the Bourbon, you can, if you have to, make this alcohol-free. In which case the ice cream will need to stand a little once out of the freezer before you serve it.

I must also tell you that this is quite magnificent with the sticky toffee sauce on p.216. Just make sure the sauce is at room temperature before you pour it over the ice cream.

During the holidays, I make this with brandy in place of Bourbon.

For make ahead/store notes see p.279

Caramel (not regular) sweetened condensed milk or dulce de leche – 1 x 14-ounce can (1⅓ cups)
Heavy cream – 1¼ cups
Sea salt flakes – 1–2 teaspoons or ½–1 teaspoon fine sea salt
Bourbon or brandy – 1–3 tablespoons

To serve:
Pecan nuts

2 x 1 pint airtight containers

1   Scrape the caramel condensed milk or dulce de leche into the bowl of a freestanding mixer or, if you're using an electric hand whisk, just into a large bowl, then add the cream and 1 teaspoon of the salt and whisk until it thickens.

2   Taste to see if it's salty enough for you, remembering that the saltiness will be slightly muted (as will the sweetness) once it's frozen. If you want more salt (and I always do) add to taste and begin whisking slowly while gradually adding half the Bourbon. Taste again to see if you want to add the rest of the Bourbon. If so, pour in, whisking gently. I usually end up using all 3 tablespoons.

3   Give a good fold by hand, using a silicone spatula, then decant into your containers and put into the freezer for 8 hours or overnight.

4   This ice cream is fairly soft-serve, and will be softer the more Bourbon you use, so there's no need to let it stand out of the freezer before serving, either as it is, or sprinkled with chopped pecans.

EMERGENCY BROWNIES

MAKES 2 GENEROUS
SQUARES OR 4 MORE
MODEST RECTANGLES

Unsalted butter – 3 tablespoons, soft

Light brown sugar – ¼ cup

Maple or light corn syrup –
1 tablespoon

All-purpose flour – 3 tablespoons

Unsweetened cocoa powder – 3
tablespoons

Sea salt flakes – ¼ teaspoon or
⅛ teaspoon fine sea salt

Egg – 1 large, at room temperature

Vanilla extract – 1 teaspoon

Walnut pieces – ½ cup

Chocolate chips – ¼ cup, dark or milk,
as wished

**1 x approx. 7 x 4 x 2 inches
aluminum foil pan**

This is for those times you urgently need a brownie, but don't want to make – or, rather, can't justify making – a whole batch. This recipe makes two (four if needs be) fudgy brownies to be snaffled straight from the pan. And they can be turned into glorious sundaes: squodge into glasses with ice cream, pour a little maple syrup over, and sprinkle with chopped walnuts.

It is worth keeping takeout aluminum foil pans in the house just to make these. Take my word for it, it will be a frequent occurrence.

For make ahead/store notes see p.279

1   Preheat the oven to 325°F. Put the butter, sugar, and maple or light corn syrup into a small heavy-based saucepan and gently warm, stirring once or twice, until the butter's melted and the sugar has dissolved. Remove the pan from the heat.

2   Fork together the flour, cocoa, and salt to mix, then beat into the butter and sugar pan with a wooden spoon or spatula until smoothly combined.

3   Whisk the egg with the vanilla – just casually, by hand – then stir into the pan, giving a final little whisk, if needed, to make sure everything's mixed together thoroughly, before folding in the nuts and chocolate chips. Pour and scrape this nubbly brownie batter into an aluminum foil pan measuring approx. 7 x 4 x 2 inches. Bake in the oven for 15–20 minutes until it is beginning to come away at the sides and the top has dried a little just around the edges.

4   Transfer to a wire rack and let cool – but not completely. I leave them for 20–30 minutes (and that's difficult enough) so that my first bite gets them when still warm, but just set enough to cut into 2 squidgy squares. If your need is not so great, or you want them to go further, cut each square in half again.

PEAR, PISTACHIO, AND ROSE CAKE

This is a delicately perfumed confection: yes, a cake, but no ordinary cake; the fruit keeps it so tender and damp that it's as if it's been drenched in light, scented syrup. I've been bold with the amount of rosewater here but, with the pears and pistachios, it strikes only the most fluttering of floral notes. True, the amount of rose petals I strew on top makes it look as if you might just as well wear it on your head as eat it, but it's the sort of cake that invites exuberance.

For make ahead/store notes see p.279

For make ahead/store notes see p.279

1 Preheat the oven to 350°F. Grease the sides and line the base of your springform cake pan with parchment paper.

2 Put the sugar and ¾ cup of pistachios into a food processor and blitz until the pistachios are finely ground, with a few nubbly bits, too.

3 Add the remaining cake ingredients and blitz until everything is smoothly combined and the pears have been puréed into the batter. Remove the blade, scrape down the mixture, and use the spatula to help ease every bit of batter into the prepared pan.

4 Bake for 40–50 minutes, though take a look at 35 and if the cake looks like it's browning too fast, loosely cover with aluminum foil. When the cake's ready, it will be brown on top, beginning to come away at the edges, and a cake tester will come out with just a few damp crumbs sticking to it.

5 Sit the cake on a wire rack and leave to cool completely in the pan; like all flourless cakes, it will sink a little. When the cake is completely cold, unclip, remove the base, and transfer to a cake stand or plate.

6 Mix the preserves, lemon juice, and rosewater together in a cup, then brush this glaze over the surface of the cake, removing any small blobs of apricot if there are any. Scatter with finely chopped pistachios and strew with rose petals, then sprinkle a few more pistachio crumbs on the top.

For the cake:
Vegetable oil – for greasing
Sugar – 1 cup
Shelled pistachios – ¾ cup
Thin-skinned pears, such as Bartlett (not too ripe) – 1 pound (approx. 3), cored and cut into chunks, skin still on
Fine almond flour – 2 cups
Baking powder (gluten-free if required) – 1½ teaspoons
Eggs – 6 large, at room temperature
Rosewater – 1½ teaspoons

For the topping:
Apricot preserves – 2 teaspoons
Lemon – ½ teaspoon of juice
Rosewater – ½ teaspoon

To decorate:
Chopped pistachios
Edible rose petals

1 x 9-inch springform cake pan

CUMIN SEED CAKE

CUTS INTO 12 SLICES

Cumin seeds – 4 teaspoons
All-purpose flour – 2⅓ cups
Baking powder – 2 teaspoons
Unsalted butter – 2 sticks (16 tablespoons), soft
Sugar – 1 cup, plus 1 teaspoon
Orange – 1, finely grated zest
Orange blossom water – 2 teaspoons
Eggs – 3 large, at room temperature
Whole milk – 3 tablespoons, at room temperature

1 x 2-pound loaf pan, approx.
10 x 5 x 3 inches

It occurred to me – while cleaning out my spice drawer, a task I soon abandoned – that it might be interesting to use cumin in place of the caraway in a traditional seed cake. It really works: the toasted cumin gives a subtle spiciness but does nothing to rupture the calm of a classic plain cake.

Interestingly, caraway did used to be known as Persian cumin, and in many languages both cumin and caraway are known by the same name. Some ideas are just meant to be…

For make ahead/store notes see p.279

1   Toast the cumin seeds in a dry, hot frying pan, until their earthy aroma wafts up: keep watch over your pan, as you don't want the seeds to burn. Transfer to a plate to cool. Mix the flour and baking powder together, then set that aside, too.

2   Preheat the oven to 325°F and put a paper liner into your loaf pan, or line the base and sides with parchment paper.

3   Beat together the butter, the 1 cup of sugar, and the orange zest until light and fluffy. Beat in the orange blossom water and then, at a slightly lower speed, about a third of the flour mixture. Once it is incorporated, beat in one of the eggs until it too is incorporated and continue in this vein until both flour and eggs are finished.

4   Give a good scrape down to mix in any flour clinging to the sides of the bowl then, still gently, beat in the milk and the cooled toasted cumin seeds. Finally, give everything a good stir with a wooden spoon, making sure there are no speckles of flour remaining, and gently dollop the stiff batter into the lined pan.

5   Smooth the top, sprinkle the teaspoon of sugar over, and bake in the oven for 50–60 minutes, or until a cake tester comes out clean and the cake has a beautiful, golden-crackled top. Place on a wire rack and let the cake cool completely before removing from its pan.

LEMON TENDERCAKE
WITH BLUEBERRY COMPOTE

When I was in the Mud Pie café in Kansas City, I ate more of their mini lemon bundt cakes than a human being should be able to manage in one sitting. But I can't tell you how easy it was. Oh, and did I say they were vegan? As is this. The café gave me their recipe, but I have played fast and loose with it, and turned it into a tender sponge, to be topped with coconut-milk yogurt and – like a retro cheesecake topping – blueberry compote.

This cake has a miraculous texture – almost like a super-aerated fluffy pancake – and a delicate flavor; it is scented with lemon rather than tingling with it. And even though there is coconut milk in the cake, this comes through as sweetness rather than tropical exuberance. The coconut makes itself more noticeable in the yogurt topping, though still mildly. And for all that it is a tripartite affair, it is ridiculously easy to make: the perfect dessert when friends come round for supper.

Don't shake the can of coconut milk, as it's best to get as much of the thick creamy part as possible. However, please don't worry too much about it: the better-quality cans of coconut milk tend to be thicker anyway. But you are not allowed even to think about using light coconut milk.

For make ahead/store notes see p.279

1   Preheat the oven to 350°F. Grease the sides and line the base of your springform cake pan with parchment paper.

2   Combine the flour, baking powder, baking soda, and salt in a bowl large enough to take all the other ingredients later.

3   In a wide pitcher (or another bowl), whisk the oil, sugar, and coconut milk together, followed by the lemon zest and juice and the vanilla extract.

4   Pour the pitcher of liquid ingredients into the bowl of dry ingredients, whisking to combine, then pour into the prepared pan and bake for 30–35 minutes, by which time the top will be golden brown, the sides shrinking away from the pan and a cake tester should come out clean. Transfer to a wire rack and leave the cake to cool completely in its pan. It may sink slightly as it cools, but this need not concern you in the slightest. While you're waiting, you can get on with making the blueberry compote.

(continued)

For the cake:
All-purpose flour – 1¾ cups
Baking powder – 1½ teaspoons
Baking soda – ½ teaspoon
Fine sea salt – ¼ teaspoon
Vegetable oil – ⅔ cup, plus more for greasing
Sugar – ¾ cup
Coconut milk – 1 cup plus 2 tablespoons (see recipe introduction)
Lemons – 2, finely grated zest, plus 3 tablespoons of juice
Vanilla extract – 1 teaspoon

For the compote:
Blueberries – 1 cup
Lemon – 1 tablespoon of juice
Sugar – 1 tablespoon
Cold water – 3 tablespoons, plus 1½ teaspoons
Cornstarch – 1½ teaspoons

For the topping:
Plain coconut-milk yogurt – 1 cup
Vanilla extract – 1 teaspoon
Confectioners' sugar – 2½ teaspoons

1 x 8-inch springform cake pan

5   Put the blueberries, lemon juice, sugar, and the 3 tablespoons of cold water into a saucepan and bring to a boil, then turn down the heat and simmer, stirring gently every now and again, for a couple of minutes until the blueberries have softened in the now garnet-glossy liquid.

6   Take the pan off the heat and, in a small cup, mix the cornstarch with the 1½ teaspoons of cold water and stir this paste into the pan of blueberries, making sure you scrape every last bit out. Stir together, put the pan back over the heat, and stir gently for about 30 seconds, by which time the sauce will have started bubbling again and will have thickened. If you feel it has become too jam-like and thick, simply add a little more water and stir it in over the heat. Pour the compote into a small heatproof bowl or pitcher to let it cool. It will set once cold.

7   Do not assemble the cake until just before serving. So: unclip the completely cold cake from its pan, unmold it, and turn it over (so the underneath is now on top) onto a cake stand or plate.

8   Mix the coconut-milk yogurt and vanilla together, spoon the confectioners' sugar into a tea-strainer, then sift it over the yogurt and stir it in, too, before spreading and swirling this soft mixture over the top of the cake. Thrash the blueberry compote a little with a fork to loosen it, and gently spoon it on top, leaving a gleaming white frame. Serve immediately.

VICTORIA SPONGE
WITH CARDAMOM, MARMALADE, AND CRÈME FRAÎCHE

There are few finer cakes to eat for afternoon tea than a Victoria Sponge, and I have made many in my time. This is the first time, however, that I have thought to change anything other than the preserves I use, and I am totally won over by this exotically scented and bitter-edged version, however immodest that sounds. The cardamom in the cake and the marmalade used to sandwich it seemed to cry out for the tang of crème fraîche rather than the traditional whipped cream.

I think it's worth seeking out ground cardamom here, just because it is difficult to crush the seeds fine enough – I am a lazy person – but it is a preference, not a diktat. If you are using cardamom seeds you've pounded yourself, then use – once they're ground – half the amount of the ready-ground, as they are much headier and would otherwise overwhelm.

For make ahead/store notes see p.279

For make ahead/store notes see p.279

For the cake:
Unsalted butter – 2 sticks (16 tablespoons), soft, plus more for greasing
Superfine sugar – 1 cup plus 2 tablespoons, plus 1 teaspoon
Orange – 1 small, finely grated zest, plus 2–3 tablespoons of juice
All-purpose flour – 1⅔ cups
Cornstarch – 3 tablespoons
Baking powder – 2½ teaspoons
Ground cardamom – 1 teaspoon
Eggs – 4 large, at room temperature

For the filling:
Bitter marmalade – ¼ cup, or as desired
Crème fraîche – ⅔ cup

2 x 8-inch cake pans

1   Preheat the oven to 350°F. Grease the sides and line the bases of your cake pans with parchment paper.

2   Beat the butter, the 1 cup plus 2 tablespoons sugar, and orange zest together until very light and fluffy.

3   Measure the flour, cornstarch, baking powder, and ground cardamom into another bowl and stir to combine.

4   Beat 1 egg into the creamed butter and sugar, followed by 1 tablespoon of the flour mixture, and go on in this manner until all 4 eggs are used up. Give a good scrape down and then gently and gradually beat in the rest of the flour mixture.

5   Once everything's smoothly combined, start beating in the orange juice, one cautious tablespoon at a time (you may need only 2) until your batter drops easily off the beater when lifted up out of the bowl.

6   Divide the cake batter evenly between the lined cake pans and smooth the tops. Place side by side in the oven and bake for 20–25 minutes, or until the deep-gold tops of the cakes are springy to the touch and a cake tester comes out clean.

7   Take them out of the oven and leave on a wire rack for 10 minutes before turning them out. I rather like the checkerboard indentations the rack makes, but if you don't, line the wire rack with parchment paper to stop it leaving so much of an impression on what will be the top of your cake.

8   Once the cakes are cooled, put the thickest one top-side down onto a cake stand or plate. Stir the marmalade to soften it, then spread it on top of the cake, pushing it right to the edges. It may seem like a mean layer but if you're using a good bitter marmalade, you won't need any more. Should you be using a less intense, fine-cut marmalade you might want to add more.

9   Spread the crème fraîche over the marmalade, easing it out to the very edges of the cake so that it will begin to ooze out a little once the top goes on.

10 Put the other cake on, flat-side down, and then sprinkle with the teaspoon of sugar to give the cake a light dusting.

CHOCOLATE CAKE
WITH COFFEE BUTTERCREAM

This is a reassuringly easy cake to make, requiring nothing more taxing than beating wet ingredients into dry: in other words, just a bowl-and-wooden-spoon number.

And while you certainly don't need a processor to make the simple coffee buttercream, I loathe sifting, and this gets round the necessity of doing so. If you are making it by hand, however, sift the confectioners' sugar and beat with the butter until soft, before gently stirring in the hot coffee, to give you a smooth buff-colored icing.

For make ahead/store notes see p.279

1   Preheat the oven to 350°F and grease the sides and line the bases of your cake pans.

2   Combine the flour, sugar, cocoa, 2 teaspoons of instant espresso powder, baking powder, and baking soda in a large pitcher (for ease of pouring later) or bowl and fork together until thoroughly combined. Whisk the milk, oil, and eggs together in another pitcher, though it can be a much smaller one. Pour these wet ingredients into the dry ones and, just with a wooden spoon or a little hand whisk if you prefer, beat to mix until you have a smooth, but fudgily thick mixture. Finally, and gently, beat in the just-boiled water, making sure to scrape the bottom of the pitcher well as you stir and fold. When you have a smooth, dark, glossy, and now fairly runny batter, pour equally into the two pans.

3   Put these well-filled pans into the oven and bake for 25–35 minutes – though start checking at 20 – by which time the cakes should be coming away from the edges of the pans, feel firm to the touch on top, and a cake tester will come out all but clean. Don't worry if they've cracked a little on top.

4   Stand the cooked cakes in their pans on a wire rack for 15 minutes, before unmolding gently and peeling off the lining; proceed carefully as these are tender sponges. Let them cool completely before frosting.

5   To make the buttercream, pulse the confectioners' sugar a good few times in the processor to get rid of any lumps, then add the butter and blitz to mix, scraping down the bowl once or twice.

For the cake:
All-purpose flour – 1¾ cups
Sugar – 1⅓ cups
Unsweetened cocoa powder – ¾ cup, sifted if lumpy
Instant espresso powder – 2 teaspoons
Baking powder – 2 teaspoons
Baking soda – 1 teaspoon
Whole milk – ¾ cup, at room temperature
Vegetable oil – ¾ cup, plus more for greasing
Eggs – 2 large, at room temperature
Water from a freshly boiled kettle – 1 cup

For the buttercream:
Confectioners' sugar – 3½ cups
Unsalted butter – 1½ sticks (12 tablespoons), soft
Instant espresso powder – 2½ teaspoons, dissolved in 1 tablespoon just-boiled water

To decorate:
Chocolate-covered coffee beans

2 x 8-inch cake pans

With the motor running again, pour the coffee down the funnel of the processor. Remove the blade, and use a large, bendy spatula to make sure everything is scraped down and combined.

6   Sit the thicker of the two cakes on a plate or stand, flat-side up. Spread generously with about half of the coffee buttercream, then sandwich with the other cake, top-side up. Pile the rest of the buttercream on top, and use a small cranked spatula to spread it, swirlingly, over the cake. Decorate with chocolate-covered coffee beans, however you so wish. I favor a shiny-beaded necklace effect, as you can see.

VANILLA LAYER CAKE
WITH ERMINE ICING

If a cartoon character were thinking about a cake, this is the one that would appear in the thought bubble above her or his head. Or, as a friend of my daughter's said, when you think about wanting to eat cake, this is the cake you want to eat. It is very much in the old-fashioned American diner style: a majestic creation, slathered in fluffy, super-sweet buttercream icing.

I have to say, this method of making buttercream was a revelation to me. I came across it on a website that I am slightly obsessed with, Serious Eats, where it rather undersells itself as "flour buttercream." On further investigation, I found it is also known as hot milk buttercream or, more gloriously, ermine icing. I know that starting off with a gluey flour-paste doesn't sound an appealing way to go about it, but this roux method creates the lightest, moussiest buttercream you could imagine. Since the roux has to be completely cold before being whipped into the butter, I'd advise making this part well in advance, then actually finishing off the buttercream once the cakes have cooled.

And those of you who are inclined to be disparaging about the idea of adding vegetable shortening to a cake should know that this is what helps create a gorgeously fluffy sponge, best eaten on the day it's made, though no hardship after.

For me this cake is all about its pale vanilla splendor, but I admit that were I making this for a child's birthday party, I would add a vulgar note with a confetti-covering of sprinkles.

For make ahead/store notes see p.279

1   Start with the frosting base: in a wide-ish saucepan (I use one of 9 inches diameter), whisk together the flour and sugar, then slowly whisk in the milk. Put the pan over a medium-low heat and, whisking continuously, bring to a boil, then let it cook, still whisking assiduously until it's thickened and lost its overtly floury taste. This shouldn't take more than a minute or two from boiling. Take the pan off the heat, whisk for 30 seconds, then scrape the thick paste into a shallow bowl and press a piece of plastic wrap directly on the surface of this admittedly not terribly attractive mixture. Leave it to cool – this will probably take 1½–2 hours – then stick the bowl in the fridge to make sure it's properly cold when called into service later, though to speed the process you could just put it straight in the fridge while still hot.

2   To make the cakes, preheat the oven to 350°F. Grease the sides and line the bases of your cake pans with parchment paper.

3   Pour the milk into a pitcher and stir in the lemon juice. Leave this to one side for a moment and, with an electric mixer (for ease), beat the butter and shortening until pale and creamy. Still beating, add the sugar, a tablespoonful at a time, until you have a light fluffy mixture in front of you. Still beating, add the eggs, one at a time, making sure each one is incorporated before adding the next. Give the bowl a good scrape down.

4   Mix the flour, baking powder, baking soda, and salt together in a bowl and, more gently now, beat a third of this into the cake batter, followed by a third of the lemon-soured-milk, and continue until both are used up. Beat in the vanilla extract, give a good fold and scrape by hand, then divide between the prepared cake pans.

5   Bake for 20–25 minutes until the cakes are golden brown and coming away at the sides, the surface feels springy, and a cake tester comes out clean. Leave the pans on a wire rack for 15 minutes before carefully turning out; go gently as these are tender babies. Peel off the lining from the base (now uppermost) and leave to cool.

6   So, when the paste's cold and the cakes are ditto, you can carry on with the frosting. Using either a freestanding mixer or an electric hand whisk, duly whisk the butter for 2 minutes or so, scraping the bowl down regularly, until it's smooth, creamy, and pale. Do not stint on this part: you want it really whipped. Whisk in the cold

For the frosting base:
All-purpose flour – ⅓ cup
Sugar – 1 cup
Whole milk – 1 cup

For the cake:
Whole milk – ⅔ cup, at room temperature
Lemon – 1 teaspoon of juice
Unsalted butter – 1 stick (8 tablespoons), soft, plus more for greasing
Vegetable shortening – 6 tablespoons
Sugar – 1 cup plus 2 tablespoons
Eggs – 3 large, at room temperature
All-purpose flour – 1¾ cups
Baking powder – 1 teaspoon
Baking soda – ½ teaspoon
Fine sea salt – a pinch
Vanilla extract – 2½ teaspoons

To finish the frosting:
Unsalted butter – 2 sticks (16 tablespoons), soft
Fine sea salt – a pinch
Vanilla extract – 2½ teaspoons

2 x 8-inch cake pans

paste, a tablespoon at a time, mixing well between each spoonful and making sure it's properly combined before adding the next one. You will – again – need to do a bit of scraping down from time to time. Once you've used up the paste, add the salt and the vanilla extract and carry on whisking for a good 3 minutes – still on scraping-down duty – until the mixture has increased in volume and you have an impressively light and creamy buttercream in front of you.

7   If one of the cakes is fatter than the other, use that one as the bottom layer and sit it on your cake stand or plate, flat-side up, then spread just under a third of the buttercream on top; a small cranked spatula is my tool of choice for this work. Sandwich with the other cake, flat-side down, and spread half the remaining frosting on top, smoothing it to cover it entirely, then swirl delicately away, unless you have the patience, dexterity, and desire to give this cake a smooth, hat-box finish. Smooth the rest of the frosting around the edges so that the cake is completely covered. Here, even I attempt a smooth look, though often with only qualified success.

8   I am quite cavalier about leaving the cake out of the fridge for a few hours before serving (as long as the weather isn't hot) as I find refrigerating it gives the sponge a heavier, denser texture, though no doubt health and safety regulations would advise against. Your risk, your call.

GINGER AND WALNUT CARROT CAKE

This is very different from the richly sweet, loftily layered and aerated American original. While it is in some senses far more reminiscent of an old-fashioned, slightly rustic British teatime treat, it is, with its ginger-spiked cream cheese icing – only on top, not running through the middle as well – just right to bring to the table, in dessert guise, at the end of dinner, too.

Before you chop the amber dice of crystallized ginger, rub the cubes between your fingers to remove excess sugar. Then chop them finely, though not obsessively so: you want small nuggets, not a sticky clump. And, for what it's worth, I find it easier to crumble up the walnuts with my fingers, rather than chopping them on a board.

For make ahead/store notes see p.279

1　Preheat the oven to 325°F and grease the sides and line the base of your springform cake pan with parchment paper.

2　Put the flour, baking powder, baking soda, ground ginger, and salt into a bowl and fork well to mix thoroughly.

3　Beat the sugar, eggs, and oil in another large bowl until they are completely mixed together, then gradually add the flour mixture, scraping the bowl you're beating them in to rescue and incorporate any flour clinging to the edges. At this stage the mixture may seem alarmingly stiff, but the carrots will loosen it up. So, beat in the carrots and then fold in the 1 cup of prepared walnuts and 4½ tablespoons chopped crystallized ginger, until everything is evenly combined.

4　Spoon and scrape into the prepared pan. Don't worry if it looks as if you haven't got nearly enough batter, as the cake will rise well as it bakes. Smooth the top and put in the oven (this is when to make the frosting, see step 5) for 45–55 minutes. When it's ready, the cake will be set and golden brown on top, beginning to shrink away from the edges of the pan, and a cake tester will come out with just a few crumbs stuck to it. Transfer to a wire rack and leave to cool in its pan.

5　As soon as the cake's in the oven, get on with the frosting. Beat the butter and confectioners' sugar together and when creamily combined, beat in the cornstarch, followed by half the cream cheese.

CUTS INTO 8–12 SLICES

For the cake:
All-purpose flour – 1⅔ cups
Baking powder – 1 teaspoon
Baking soda – ½ teaspoon
Ground ginger – 2 teaspoons
Fine sea salt – ¼ teaspoon
Light brown sugar – ¾ cup plus 2 tablespoons
Eggs – 2 large, at room temperature
Vegetable oil – ¾ cup plus 1 tablespoon, plus more for greasing
Carrots – 7 ounces (2 medium), peeled and coarsely grated, to give 1¾ cups loosely packed
Walnut pieces – 1 cup, roughly chopped or crumbled
Crystallized ginger – 4½ tablespoons, finely chopped

For the frosting:
Unsalted butter – 7 tablespoons, soft
Confectioners' sugar – 1 cup, sifted if lumpy
Cornstarch – 1 teaspoon
Cream cheese – 4 ounces (7 tablespoons), fridge-cold
Fresh ginger – 1 tablespoon coarsely grated

To decorate:
Walnut pieces – ¼ cup, roughly chopped or crumbled
Crystallized ginger – 1½ tablespoons finely chopped

1 x 8-inch springform cake pan

Once that's incorporated, beat in the remaining half. Be careful at all times not to over-beat or the frosting will get too runny. Starting with the grated ginger on a plate, get out a piece of paper towel and, moving quickly, spoon the grated ginger into the center, bring up the edges of the paper, holding them together to form a little swag bag, and press on it over the bowl to squeeze out the intense ginger juice. Beat this into the frosting in its bowl. Cover with plastic wrap and refrigerate.

6   When the cake is completely cold, take the frosting out of the fridge for about 20 minutes, by which time it will have softened to a still thick but spreadable consistency. Beat briefly to help this along, and make sure it's smooth. Unclip and release the cake from its pan, unmolding it, and sit it on a cake stand or plate. Spread the frosting on top, swirling it a little, then sprinkle the chopped walnuts and ginger on top.

RASPBERRY-FLECKED SOUR CREAM CAKE

This – for all its prettiness, just falling on the acceptable side of cute – is a modest, plain cake, perfect for slicing and eating with a cup of tea or coffee. The sour cream makes for a firm but velvety soft crumb, and the freeze-dried raspberries that are folded into the batter punctuate it with sharpness. Do not be tempted to substitute fresh raspberries here. I have found freeze-dried raspberries easily at the supermarket; I hope you will be as lucky.

Should you not have the 9-inch savarin ring mold, then you could bake this in a 1-pound loaf pan.

For make ahead/store notes see p.279

1   Preheat the oven to 350°F. Grease your savarin ring mold generously with oil using a pastry brush, and leave the pan upside-down over a piece of newspaper or parchment paper while you get on with making the cake batter. Or line a loaf pan.

2   Mix the flour, baking powder, and baking soda in a bowl. Put the sour cream into a large measuring jug, add the sugar, eggs, vanilla, and oil and whisk to mix.

3   Add the wet ingredients to the dry ones and beat until you've got a smooth batter. Fold in the freeze-dried raspberries, then pour the mixture into the prepared mold (or loaf pan) and bake for 30–35 minutes (or 45–50 minutes if using a loaf pan) until the cake is risen and golden brown and a cake tester pronged into two parts of the cake comes out clean. Sit the cake in its pan on a wire rack until cool before turning out, easing it gently with a small spatula first.

4   Once the cake's completely cold, transfer to a cake stand or plate. Mix the confectioners' sugar with the freshly boiled water, adding 1 teaspoon at a time, until you have a thick but still pourable consistency; I find 4 teaspoons of water generally does it. Make sure there are no lumps before you spoon it over the top of the cake and sprinkle immediately with freeze-dried raspberries.

CUTS INTO 16 SLICES, BUT IT WOULD BE VERY EASY TO EAT 3 OR 4 AT A SITTING

For the cake:
All-purpose flour – 1¾ cups
Baking powder – ½ teaspoon
Baking soda – ½ teaspoon
Sour cream – ¾ cup, at room temperature
Sugar – ¾ cup
Eggs – 2 large, at room temperature
Vanilla extract – 1 teaspoon
Vegetable oil – ½ cup, plus more for greasing the savarin ring mold
Freeze-dried raspberries – 3 tablespoons, plus more for sprinkling

For the frosting:
Confectioners' sugar – 1¼ cups, sifted if lumpy
Water from a freshly boiled kettle – 1–2 tablespoons

1 x 9-inch non-stick savarin ring mold or 1 x 1-pound loaf pan approx. 7½ x 5 x 3 inches

SCENTED CITRUS CAKE

Created for a gluten-free friend's birthday, this is a wonderfully uplifting cake: subtly fragrant but full of zing.

If you can't get ground cardamom – though do try to, I consider it a baking essential – you can pound your own, but it'll be much stronger; so here you would need only ½ teaspoon.

For make ahead/store notes see p.280

For the cake:
Unsalted butter – 1½ sticks (12 tablespoons), soft, plus more for greasing
Sugar – 1 cup
Lemons – 1–2, finely grated zest of 1, plus 3 tablespoons of juice
Orange – 1, finely grated zest, plus 2 tablespoons of juice
Eggs – 4 large, at room temperature
Rice flour – ½ cup
Ground cardamom – 1 teaspoon
Orange flower water – 2 teaspoons
Lime – 2 tablespoons of juice
Fine almond flour – 2 cups
Baking powder (gluten-free if required) – 1 teaspoon

For the glacé icing:
Lemon – 1 tablespoon of juice
Lime – 1 teaspoon of juice
Orange – 1 tablespoon of juice
Confectioners' sugar – 1½ cups, sifted if lumpy

1 x 9-inch springform cake pan

1 Preheat the oven to 350°F and grease the sides and line the base of your springform cake pan with parchment paper.

2 Into the bowl of a freestanding mixer (for ease), though you don't need to use one, add the butter, sugar and the zests of the lemon and the orange. Beat well until you have a pale and creamy mixture.

3 Add the eggs, beating in one at a time, at not too high a speed. Be patient doing this, letting each egg be completely mixed in before adding the next one, scraping down as you go. Don't worry if the batter starts to look curdled at any stage.

4 Once the eggs are all added, beat in the rice flour and, when that is incorporated, the ground cardamom and orange flower water, then slowly pour in the citrus juices, beating as before, followed by the almond flour and baking powder.

5 Finish off by folding and stirring everything together by hand and pour this grainy, fragrant, and utterly delicious batter (just try a bit) into the prepared pan.

6 Bake for about 35 minutes, although start checking at 30 and be prepared to go on to 40. Once ready, the cake should be coming away from the sides, just firm on top, and a cake tester will come out with only a few just-damp crumbs stuck to it.

7 Transfer to a wire rack and leave to cool completely in the pan. Unclip the pan and slide the cake off its base and onto a cake plate or stand, ready for icing. It is a damp and delicate cake, so be careful and treat it tenderly.

8 Once the cake is cold, mix the lemon, lime, and orange juices in a little bowl and put the confectioners' sugar into another bowl. Gradually add the citrus juices to the confectioners' sugar, whisking until you have a smooth and flowingly spreadable tangy icing. You may not need every last drop of juice.

9 Pour the icing on top of the cake, then very gently – I like a small cranked spatula for this – ease the icing out from the middle of the cake to spread to the edges. Don't worry – indeed, be pleased – if the icing drips down the sides a little.

SUNKEN CHOCOLATE AMARETTO CAKE
WITH CRUMBLED AMARETTI CREAM

This is one of those dark, squidgy-bellied chocolate cakes that I turn to gratefully when I have friends over to supper; a gratitude that is always reciprocated. The mixture of almonds and Amaretto gives a marzipan kick, balancing the bitterness of the chocolate.

The amaretti cream alongside brings both smoothness and a fine honeycomb crunch to the velvetiness of the cake.

For make ahead/store notes see p.280

1   Preheat the oven to 350°F and lightly grease the sides and line the base of your springform cake pan with parchment paper.

2   Put the chocolate and butter into a heatproof bowl and melt, either over a saucepan of boiling water, making sure the bowl doesn't touch the water, or in a microwave. Pour into a pitcher and leave to cool a little.

3   Whisk the eggs and sugar until thick and moussy and doubled, if not tripled, in volume. This will take 2–3 minutes, using a freestanding mixer, and 1–2 minutes longer with an electric hand whisk.

4   Fork the almond flour and cocoa together in a small bowl to mix them thoroughly. Turn the mixer speed to low and gently whisk into the eggs and sugar, tablespoon by tablespoon.

5   Stir the Amaretto liqueur into the slightly cooled, melted chocolate and butter, then pour this glossy mixture in a slow, steady stream into the cake batter, whisking all the while; it will look like a fabulous chocolate mousse. Give a final fold by hand to make sure everything is smoothly and airily combined.

6   Pour and scrape the batter into the prepared pan. Bake in the oven for 20–25 minutes until the cake is beginning to come away at the edges, the top has formed a slightly cracked and bubbled thin crust the color of pale milk chocolate – the cake will be dark and tender underneath – and a cake tester comes out with just a few damp crumbs cleaving to it.

7   Remove to a wire rack, drape a clean tea towel over the pan, and leave to cool. As it cools, the top of the cake will crack a little more, and it will sink slightly, leaving a frilly edge.

CUTS INTO 10–12 SLICES

Bittersweet chocolate, preferably 70% cocoa solids – 4 ounces, roughly chopped
Unsalted butter – 7 tablespoons, soft, cut into cubes or dolloped in teaspoons, plus more for greasing
Eggs – 4 large, at room temperature
Superfine sugar – ⅔ cup
Fine almond flour – ¾ cup
Unsweetened cocoa powder – 2 tablespoons, sifted if lumpy, plus 1 teaspoon for dusting
Amaretto liqueur – 3 tablespoons

For the amaretti cream:
Heavy cream – 1 cup
Amaretto liqueur – 1 tablespoon
Amaretti biscuits – 4, crumbled

1 8-inch springform cake pan

8   Once the cake is cold, unclip the pan, and gently lift the cake out
    – remove the base only if you are very brave – onto a cake stand
    or plate. Press the teaspoon of cocoa through a fine tea strainer to
    dust the top thickly, rather like the coating on a chocolate truffle.

9   Just before serving, whip the cream and Amaretto together, until
    ripples start showing on the surface and it's thickened but still soft
    enough to dollop alongside the cake. Very gently fold most of the
    crumbled amaretti biscuits into the cream, which will thicken it
    slightly more. Decant into a small serving bowl and sprinkle the
    rest of the amaretti crumbles on top.

COCONUT SNOWBALL CAKE

I first made this at Christmas, as a light, fluffy counterpoint to a traditional dark and dense fruit cake. I don't stop making it at other times of the year: I just drop the "snowball" bit.

The coconut oil in the cake batter not only gives flavor, but makes for a light and tender sponge, and the frosting – otherwise known as 7-minute-frosting – has a dreamy marshmallow texture.

For hard-core coconutters only.

For make ahead/store notes see p.280

1 Preheat the oven to 350°F and grease the sides and line the bases of your cake pans with parchment paper.

2 Combine the flour, baking powder, baking soda, salt, and unsweetened shredded coconut in a bowl and use a fork to make sure everything's thoroughly combined. Set aside for a moment.

3 Using a freestanding mixer for ease, cream the coconut oil and sugar until soft and fluffy, scraping down with a spatula as needed. Add the vanilla and continue beating as you break in the first egg.

4 When the egg has been incorporated, tip in – beating at a slightly lower speed all the while – about a third of the dry ingredients and, when also incorporated, add the second egg, and continue likewise with a further third of the dry ingredients, the final egg, and the rest of the dry ingredients. You will need to scrape down the bowl once or twice to make sure everything's been satisfactorily mixed.

5 Once you have a smooth, cohesive batter, add the coconut-milk yogurt and continue beating until that too has been incorporated. Give a final scrape down with a spatula and use it to help scrape the mixture equally between the pans, then smooth the tops before baking in the oven for 20–25 minutes. When the cakes are ready, they will be golden on top and coming away at the edges of the cake pans, and a cake tester will come out clean.

6 Remove to a wire rack and let the cakes cool in their pans for 10 minutes. Then turn them out to cool completely, covered loosely with a clean tea towel.

CUTS INTO 8–12 SLICES

For the cake:
All-purpose flour – 1½ cups
Baking powder – 2 teaspoons
Baking soda – ¼ teaspoon
Fine sea salt – a pinch
Unsweetened shredded coconut – 1 cup
Cold-pressed coconut oil – ¾ cup (needs to be solid, not runny, though not fridge-cold either), plus more for greasing
Sugar – ⅔ cup
Vanilla extract – 1 teaspoon
Eggs – 3 large, at room temperature
Coconut-milk yogurt – ¼ cup, at room temperature
Seedless raspberry preserves – ¼ cup
Lime – a spritz of juice

For the frosting:
Eggs – 2 large, at room temperature, whites only
Light corn syrup – ½ cup
Superfine sugar – ⅔ cup
Lemon – ½ teaspoon of juice
Fine sea salt – a pinch
Coconut extract – ¼ teaspoon

To decorate:
Unsweetened shredded coconut – 3 tablespoons

2 x 8-inch cake pans

7   Once the cake layers are cold, sit the thicker of the two cakes on a cake stand or plate, flat-side up. Mix together the raspberry preserves and spritz of lime juice in a bowl, then gently spread over the cake, not going all the way to the edges as you don't want it squidging out. Place the other cake, flat-side down, on top.

8   Put the egg whites, light corn syrup, superfine sugar, lemon juice, and salt into a decent-sized, grease-free heatproof bowl that fits over a saucepan to form a double boiler. Fill the saucepan with enough water to come just below – but not touching – the bowl when it sits on top. Bring the water to a boil, set the bowl on top, and, using an electric hand whisk, beat the mixture vigorously for 7 minutes. When it's ready, it should stand up in firm peaks like a meringue mixture. Lift the bowl off the saucepan, away from the heat, and add the coconut extract, beating it into the frosting.

9   Working fast – the frosting sets quickly – frost the top and sides of the sponge, making it swirly and textured rather than smooth, and take extra care not to pick up any red streaks of preserves when you frost the sides. But if you do, just quickly wipe it away with a piece of paper towel and carry on. Once all the cake is covered with its marshmallow icing, sprinkle with the unsweetened shredded coconut: you'll have to throw it slightly – if that makes sense – so that it sticks to the sides. When slicing the cake – if you can be bothered – wipe the knife down with a piece of damp paper towel between each cut for neatly cleaner slices.

DOUBLE CHOCOLATE AND PUMPKIN SEED COOKIES

Unsalted butter – 5 tablespoons, soft
Sugar – ½ cup
Light brown sugar – ⅓ cup
Egg – 1 large, at room temperature
Vanilla extract – 1 teaspoon
All-purpose flour – 1 cup
Unsweetened cocoa powder –
½ cup, sifted if lumpy
Baking soda – 1 teaspoon
Fine sea salt – ⅛ teaspoon
Bittersweet chocolate chips – ⅔ cup
Pumpkin seeds – ⅓ cup

I've eaten a great many chocolate cookies over the years – and, indeed, created a fair number of recipes for them – but there's always room for another one. And this may well be my favorite (so far).

If you like your chocolate salted – as I very much do – add somewhere between ¼ and ½ teaspoon of sea salt flakes to the cookie dough, and sprinkle another ¼–½ teaspoon sea salt over the formed cookies, just before they go into the oven. It might be wise to start with the smaller amount – not everyone has as salty a tooth as I do.

For make ahead/store notes see p.280

1   Preheat the oven to 350°F. Beat together the butter and sugars until paler in color and fluffy.

2   Add the egg and vanilla and beat to combine, scraping down the bowl to rescue and incorporate any batter clinging to the sides.

3   In another bowl, use a fork to mix together the flour, cocoa, baking soda, and salt. Gradually add to the creamed mixture in the bowl, beating it in gently.

4   With a spoon or spatula, fold in the chocolate chips and pumpkin seeds; you will have a thick, firm mixture.

5   Line a couple of baking sheets with parchment paper, then, using a heaping tablespoon measure for ease, form heaped mounds, leaving about 2½ inches space between them, easing the mixture out of the spoon with a small spatula onto the sheet. Don't flatten them.

6   Cook a batch at a time (or just bake half and freeze the other half, ready-formed to bake another day – see p.280) for 10–12 minutes, by which time the surface will feel just set and be cracked in parts. They will still feel pretty soft but will firm up as they cool. Once they're out of the oven, leave on the baking sheet for 5 minutes before transferring to a wire rack to cool a little before diving in. Or leave to cool entirely if preferred.

FORGOTTEN COOKIES

These little cookies – described by one friend as tasting like a cookie within a cookie – are really a mixture between a meringue and a cookie. Hence they've become known at home, where they're immensely popular, as Merookies, and are ideal with a cup of coffee after dinner.

I always use ready-ground cardamom, as the amount you need is pretty much impossible to grind finely enough yourself (you'd need only ⅛ of a teaspoon if using home-ground cardamom). And it is really worth seeking out mini chocolate chips, as I find regular-sized ones can spill out of the cloud-like mixture as you form them on the baking sheet.

They are called "forgotten" as, just like the Forgotten Pudding in *Nigella Express*, they are not baked, but put in a hot oven, which you immediately turn off, leaving the cookies to bake in the fading residual heat overnight. I find it all too easy actually to forget them, and always put a Post-it sticker on the oven to remind me they're in there, so I don't burn them to a cinder by preheating the oven to cook something else in it the next day.

For make ahead/store notes see p.280

For make ahead/store notes see p.280

MAKES 12–14 MEROOKIES

Eggs – 2 large, at room temperature, whites only
Fine sea salt – a pinch
Superfine sugar – ½ cup
Cornstarch – 1 teaspoon
Cider or white wine vinegar – 1 teaspoon
Ground cardamom – ¼ teaspoon
Mini dark chocolate chips – ⅓ cup
Pistachios – ½ cup, finely chopped

1   Preheat the oven to 350°F. In a grease-free bowl, whisk together the egg whites and salt until you have soft peaks. Whisk in the sugar a little at a time until thick and gleaming.

2   By hand, fold in the cornstarch, vinegar, and cardamom, then add the chocolate chips and most of the pistachios and very gently fold these in too.

3   With a spoon, drop mounded blobs of the mixture, 1½–2 inches in diameter, onto a large baking sheet lined with parchment paper. Sprinkle with the remaining pistachios.

4   Put the cookies into the oven, shut the door, and turn off the oven immediately. Let the cookies sit in the turned-off oven overnight.

NEGRONI SBAGLIATO

The classic Negroni is made with Campari, red vermouth, and gin. This one, more of a Negroni spritz, using prosecco in place of the gin, is said to have been created by happy accident at the Bar Basso in Milan in the '60s. The story may well be apocryphal, but cocktails always come with the romance of their own narrative. *Sbagliato* (roughly pronounced "sbalyato") means mistaken in Italian, so this is best translated as Messed-Up Negroni.

I mess it up even more by changing the proportions (the original version being equal amounts of all three elements) and by serving it in a pitcher rather than making it up as individual cocktails.

So, for 1 bottle of chilled prosecco, I add 1⅓ cups of Campari and ¾ cup of best-quality red vermouth. And if you can keep these bottles in the fridge too, so much the better. Mix in a pitcher, throw in some orange slices, and add ice to the glasses that you're pouring the cocktail into.

It is not advisable to make ahead/store

TURMERIC AND GINGER VODKA

This golden, deep-spiced vodka will revolutionize your Bloody Marys, and provides a warming mellow shot on its own. Pour 750ml of vodka (keep the bottle it's come in) into a wide-necked bottle or jar. Cut a 3-inch piece of fresh ginger and 3 x 3½-inch pieces of fresh turmeric into thinnish coins and add them to the vodka along with 2 teaspoons of black peppercorns. Make sure the bottle or jar is sealed properly and give it a shake, then leave in a cool, dark place for two weeks, giving it a shake anytime you happen to be passing. Then strain into a pitcher and pour back into the original vodka bottle. If you want to give this as a present, you can pour it into something a little prettier, of course.

Don't worry if there are flecks of ginger or turmeric left in the vodka; the only reason to strain it is to stop the flavors intensifying too overwhelmingly. If you want your vodka to pack more of a punch, there's nothing to stop you leaving the turmeric, ginger, and peppercorns in it for longer. Similarly, if you want to make more, you could double the amount of vodka, leaving the turmeric, ginger, and peppercorns as they are, and just let it infuse for double the time. In all cases, you will have to pour out a little to sip every few days to monitor how the flavorings are developing, but this is not necessarily an unwelcome step.

For make ahead/store notes see p.280

DIRTY LEMON MARTINI

I have always wanted to be the sort of person who drinks a dirty martini, but I just can't do it. I'm a strictly straight-up-with-a-twist woman. This is my take on it, then, though inspiration comes, originally, from Sabrina Ghayour's *Sirocco*. The brine from a jar of olives is replaced with the juice from a jar of preserved lemons; result: a fragrant, killer cocktail. So, to make one dirty lemon martini, tumble a handful of ice into a cocktail shaker along with 2 shots of gin or vodka, ½ shot of best-quality dry white vermouth, and 1 teaspoon of juice from a jar of preserved lemons. Shake well, pour into a chilled martini glass, and sip elegantly or knock back as needed.

It is not advisable to make ahead/store

GRAPEFRUIT MARGARITA

One quick gulp of a cold, sharp margarita and I feel I'm on holiday. This is not the classic version, but I have come enthusiastically to prefer it.

For one drink, squeeze a grapefruit and dip the rim of a glass into the juice (I like a tumbler, though by all means use a traditional margarita glass) and then in some lightly crushed – just with your fingers – sea salt flakes. In a cocktail shaker generously stacked with ice cubes, shake together 2 shots of tequila, 2 shots of Triple Sec, Cointreau, or other orange liqueur along with 4 shots of grapefruit juice and strain into your salt-rimmed glass, adding fresh ice cubes if you like. Spritz with lime juice to taste, for added sharpness, if wished.

And obviously, you can make pitchers of this heavenly elixir, forgoing the shaker but following the same proportions, to be poured into frosted glasses tumbled with ice.

For make ahead/store notes see p.280

MAKE AHEAD AND STORAGE NOTES

If there are no freeze notes for a recipe below, this is because it is not advisable.

16. **Waffles**
MAKE AHEAD/STORE – It is not advisable to make ahead but you can refrigerate leftovers in an airtight container for up to 3 days. Reheat on a wire rack set over a baking sheet in an oven preheated to 400°F for 4–7 minutes.
FREEZE – Freeze in an airtight container, layered with parchment paper, for up to 1 month. Reheat direct from frozen as above, allowing an extra 1–2 minutes, until crisp on the outside and piping hot all the way through.

22. **Golden Egg Curry**
MAKE AHEAD/STORE – Sauce can be made up to 3 days ahead. Cool as quickly as possible and refrigerate in an airtight container for up to 3 days. Reheat gently in a wok, stirring occasionally, until just boiling, then reduce the heat and continue with the recipe.

24. **Deviled Eggs**
MAKE AHEAD/STORE – Eggs can be made up to 1 day ahead and refrigerated in an airtight container. Sprinkle with paprika and chives just before serving. To store, do not leave at room temperature for more than 2 hours. Refrigerate leftovers in an airtight container for 1–2 days.

28. **Chili Cheese Garlic Bread**
MAKE AHEAD/STORE – The loaf can be prepared 1 day ahead. Refrigerate, wrapped in the foil, and bake for an extra 5–10 minutes.

31. **Whipped Feta Toasts**
MAKE AHEAD/STORE – Refrigerate feta mixture in an airtight container for up to 5 days. Beat briefly before using.

37. **Catalan Toasts**
MAKE AHEAD/STORE – Chop the tomato a day ahead. Store in an airtight container in the fridge and remove about an hour before serving, to let it come to room temperature. Spread on the toast just before serving.

42. **Beef and Eggplant Fatteh**
MAKE AHEAD/STORE – The pita can be toasted 1–2 days ahead. Store in an airtight container. The eggplant-meat layer can be made up to 3 days ahead. Cool and refrigerate, within two hours of cooking, in an airtight container. Return to the pan and add a splash of water, then reheat over a medium heat, stirring occasionally, until piping hot.
FREEZE – Meat layer can be frozen for up to 3 months in an airtight container. Thaw overnight in the fridge and reheat as above.

44. **Spelt Spaghetti with Spicy Sesame Mushrooms**
MAKE AHEAD/STORE – It is not advisable to make ahead but leftovers can be stored in an airtight container in the fridge for up to 3 days. Eat cold.

52. **Radiatori with Sausage and Saffron**
MAKE AHEAD/STORE – Sauce can be made up to 3 days ahead. Refrigerate, within 2 hours of making, in an airtight container. Return to a pan and reheat over a low heat, stirring occasionally, until just boiling, then continue with the recipe.
FREEZE – Sauce can be frozen in an airtight container for up to 3 months. Thaw overnight in the fridge and reheat as above.

54. **Meatballs with Orzo**
MAKE AHEAD/STORE – Meatballs and sauce can be made up to 3 days ahead. Refrigerate, within 2 hours of cooking, in an airtight container. Return to a pan and reheat gently, until just boiling. Add orzo and cook as instructed in the recipe, adding a splash of extra water if needed. Refrigerate leftovers in an airtight container for up to 3 days. Reheat in a saucepan until piping hot all the way through, adding a couple of extra splashes of water, if necessary. Do not reheat leftovers if sauce was made ahead.
FREEZE – Meatballs and sauce can be frozen for up to 3 months in an airtight container. Thaw overnight in the fridge and reheat as above.

56. **Mung Bean Dal** with Mint and Cilantro Raita
MAKE AHEAD/STORE – Refrigerate dal and raita in separate airtight containers for up to 3 days. Reheat dal in a saucepan until piping hot, adding a couple of extra splashes of water, if necessary. Reheat only once.
FREEZE – The dal only can be frozen for up to 3 months in an airtight container. Thaw overnight in the fridge and reheat as above.

59. Turmeric Rice with Cardamom and Cumin
MAKE AHEAD/STORE – It is not advisable to make ahead but you can refrigerate leftovers, within 2 hours of cooking, in an airtight container for up to 3 days. Eat cold or reheat until piping hot.

60. Carrots and Fennel with Harissa
MAKE AHEAD/STORE – It is not advisable to make ahead but you can refrigerate leftovers in an airtight container for up to 5 days.

63. Roasted Red Endive
MAKE AHEAD/STORE – It is not advisable to make ahead but you can refrigerate leftovers in an airtight container for up to 5 days.

64. Butternut and Sweet Potato Curry
MAKE AHEAD/STORE – Refrigerate cooled curry in an airtight container for up to 5 days. Reheat gently in a saucepan until piping hot. Reheat only once.
FREEZE – Leftovers can be frozen in airtight containers for up to 3 months. Thaw overnight in the fridge and reheat as above.

66. Garlic and Parmesan Mashed Potatoes
MAKE AHEAD/STORE – Refrigerate mashed potatoes, covered, for up to 3 days. Reheat gratin as directed in the recipe, or use for waffles, see p.71. Leftover gratin should not be used for waffles.

71. Potato Waffles from Leftover Garlic and Parmesan Mashed Potatoes
MAKE AHEAD/STORE – It is not advisable to make ahead but leftovers can be refrigerated on a plate covered with plastic wrap, with parchment paper between the waffles, for up to 3 days. The waffles can become soft when cold but should crisp up again on reheating. Reheat on a wire rack set over a baking sheet, in an oven preheated to 400°F for 4–7 minutes.
FREEZE – Cooked waffles can be frozen in an airtight container, layered with baking parchment, for up to 1 month. Reheat direct from frozen as above, allowing an extra 1–2 minutes, until crisp on the outside and piping hot all the way through.

72. Red Cabbage with Cranberries
MAKE AHEAD/STORE – Cool, then refrigerate in airtight containers for up to 5 days. Reheat in a saucepan until piping hot. Reheat only once.
FREEZE – In airtight containers for up to 3 months. Thaw overnight in the fridge and reheat as above.

74. Smashed Chickpeas with Garlic, Lemon, and Chile
MAKE AHEAD/STORE – It is not advisable to make ahead but you can refrigerate leftovers, within 2 hours of making, in an airtight container for up to 2 days. Eat cold.

76. Brussels Sprouts with Preserved Lemons and Pomegranate
MAKE AHEAD/STORE – It is not advisable to make ahead but you can refrigerate leftovers in an airtight container for up to 5 days. Reheat in a Dutch oven or saucepan, with a splash of water, until piping hot.

80. Moroccan Vegetable Pot
MAKE AHEAD/STORE – Refrigerate, within 2 hours of cooking, in an airtight container for up to 2 days. Reheat in a saucepan until piping hot, adding a splash of water, if necessary. Reheat only once.

FREEZE – Leftovers can be frozen in airtight containers for up to 3 months. Thaw overnight in the fridge and reheat as above.

83. Couscous with Pine Nuts and Dill
MAKE AHEAD/STORE – It is not advisable to make ahead but you can refrigerate leftovers in an airtight container for up to 3 days. Eat cold.

86. Sweet Potato Tacos with Avocado and Coriander Sauce and a Tomato and Pear Relish
MAKE AHEAD/STORE – Refrigerate sauce and relish, covered, for up to 1 day.

89. Tomato and Horseradish Salad
MAKE AHEAD/STORE – Refrigerate horseradish dressing, covered, for up to 1 week.

90. Quinoa Salad with Walnuts, Radishes, and Pomegranate
MAKE AHEAD/STORE – Refrigerate leftovers in an airtight container for up to 3 days. Salad should not be left at room temperature for more than 2 hours.

93. Radicchio, Chestnut and Blue Cheese Salad with a Citrus, Whole Grain Mustard, and Honey Dressing
MAKE AHEAD/STORE – Refrigerate dressing in a sealed container for up to 7 days. Shake before use.

94. Chopped Salad
MAKE AHEAD/STORE – It is not advisable to make ahead but you can refrigerate leftovers, in an airtight container, for up to 3 days.

96. **Beet and Goat Cheese Salad** with a Passionfruit Dressing
MAKE AHEAD/STORE – It is not advisable to make ahead but you can refrigerate leftovers in an airtight container for up to 3 days.

100. **Subverting the Spiralizer**
MAKE AHEAD/STORE – The potatoes can be cut/spiralized up to 12 hours ahead. Submerge in a large bowl of cold water and refrigerate until needed. Drain and gently pat dry with a tea towel before cooking.

103. **Spiced Almonds**
MAKE AHEAD/STORE – Make sure nuts are completely cold, then transfer to an airtight container and store in a cool, dry place for up to 2 weeks.

104. **Cilantro and Jalapeño Salsa**
MAKE AHEAD/STORE – Refrigerate in an airtight container for up to 5 days.

107. **Red-Hot Roasted Salsa**
MAKE AHEAD/STORE – Refrigerate, within 2 hours of making, in an airtight container for 5 days.
FREEZE – Can be frozen in an airtight container for up to 3 months. Thaw overnight in the fridge.

111. **White Miso Hummus**
MAKE AHEAD/STORE – Store in an airtight container in the fridge for up to 2 days.

112. **Pear and Passionfruit Chutney**
MAKE AHEAD/STORE – Store in a cool dry place for up to 1 year. Let chutney mature for 1 or 2 months before using. Once opened, refrigerate and use within 1 month.

115. **Golden Garlic Mayonnaise**
MAKE AHEAD/STORE – Refrigerate, within 2 hours of making, in an airtight container for up to 1 week.

116. **Flash-Fried Squid** with Tomato and Tequila Salsa
MAKE AHEAD/STORE – Salsa can be made 6 hours ahead. Store in an airtight container in the fridge until needed.

122. **Polenta-Fried Fish** with Minted Pea Purée
MAKE AHEAD/STORE – Leftover pea purée can be refrigerated and stored for up to 3 days, then reheated till piping hot.
FREEZE – Polenta-coated fish (if not previously frozen) can be frozen on a parchment-lined baking sheet. Once solid, transfer to a resealable plastic bag and freeze for up to 3 months. Cook direct from frozen, adding 1–2 minutes to the cooking time and check fish is cooked through before serving.

127. **Salt and Vinegar Potatoes**
MAKE AHEAD/STORE – Potatoes can be steamed up to 2 hours ahead. Refrigerate leftovers for up to 5 days and eat cold.

129. **Roast Loin of Salmon** with Aleppo Pepper and Fennel Seeds
MAKE AHEAD/STORE – It is not advisable to make ahead but you can refrigerate leftovers, within 2 hours of cooking, covered, for up to 3 days.

130. **Coconut Shrimp** with Turmeric Yogurt
MAKE AHEAD/STORE – Shrimp can be coated 3–4 hours ahead. Cover loosely with plastic wrap and refrigerate until needed.

133. **Chicken and Pea Traybake**
MAKE AHEAD/STORE – Refrigerate leftovers, within 2 hours of cooking, in an airtight container for up to 3 days. Reheat in a saucepan or microwave until piping hot all the way through.

138. **Lime and Cilantro Chicken**
MAKE AHEAD/STORE – Chicken can be marinated up to 6 hours ahead. Store in the fridge and remove 15 minutes before cooking. Refrigerate leftovers, within 2 hours of cooking, in an airtight container for up to 3 days. Eat cold.

140. **Butterflied Chicken** with Miso and Sesame Seeds
MAKE AHEAD/STORE – It is not advisable to make ahead but you can refrigerate leftovers, within 2 hours of cooking, in an airtight container for up to 3 days. Eat cold.

142. **Indian-Spiced Chicken and Potato Traybake**
MAKE AHEAD/STORE – It is not advisable to make ahead but you can refrigerate leftover chicken, within 2 hours of cooking, in an airtight container for up to 3 days. Eat cold, and see sandwich suggestion on p.142.

147. **Chicken Barley**
MAKE AHEAD/STORE – It is not advisable to make ahead but you can refrigerate leftovers, within 2 hours of cooking, in an airtight container for up to 3 days. Reheat in a saucepan, adding a splash of water if necessary, until piping hot. Reheat only once.
FREEZE – Leftovers can be frozen in an airtight container for up to 3 months. Thaw overnight in the fridge and reheat as above.

150. Chicken Fricassée with
Marsala, Chestnuts, and Thyme
MAKE AHEAD/STORE – It is not
advisable to make ahead but you can
refrigerate leftovers, within 2 hours of
cooking, in an airtight container for up
to 3 days. Reheat in a saucepan, adding
a little extra broth if needed, until piping
hot all the way through. Do not store or
reheat again if made with cooked chicken
or turkey.
FREEZE – Leftovers can be frozen for
up to 3 months in an airtight container.
Thaw overnight in the fridge and reheat as
above. Do not freeze and reheat if made
with cooked chicken or turkey.

154. Roast Duck with Orange,
Soy, and Ginger
MAKE AHEAD/STORE –
Duck can be steam roasted up to 2 days
ahead of final roasting. Make sure that
it is refrigerated within 2 hours of steam
roasting. Refrigerate leftover roasted duck
and sauce, within 2 hours of cooking,
in separate airtight containers for up to
1 day. Reheat until piping hot, or see
recipe suggestion for leftovers on p.158.
Duck fat should be transferred to an
airtight container and refrigerated for
up to 1 week.
FREEZE – Duck fat can be frozen for
up to 3 months.

160. Slow Roasted 5-Spice Lamb
with Chinese Pancakes
MAKE AHEAD/STORE – It is not
advisable to make ahead but you can
refrigerate leftover lamb, within 2 hours
of cooking, in an airtight container for
up to 3 days. Cooking juices can also be
refrigerated in a separate container for up
to 3 days.

164. Herbed Leg of Lamb
MAKE AHEAD/STORE – It is not
advisable to make ahead but you can
refrigerate leftovers, within 2 hours of
cooking, in an airtight container for up
to 3 days.

166. Cumberland Gravy
MAKE AHEAD/STORE – The gravy
can be made up to 3 days ahead. Cool
and refrigerate as quickly as possible in
an airtight container until needed. Reheat
in a saucepan over a low heat, stirring
occasionally, until just boiling. Add a
splash of extra broth if the gravy is too
thick. Reheat only once.
FREEZE – Can be frozen in an
airtight container for up to 3 months.
Thaw overnight in the fridge and
reheat as above.

168. Lamb Kofta with Garlic Sauce
MAKE AHEAD/STORE – It is not
advisable to make ahead but you can
refrigerate leftover kofta, within 2 hours
of cooking, in an airtight container for
up to 3 days. Eat cold. Leftover sauce
can be refrigerated and stored for up to
2 days in a tightly sealed container.
FREEZE – Leftover cooked and chilled
kofta can be frozen in an airtight
container for up to 1 month. Thaw
overnight in the fridge and eat cold.

171. Spiced Lamb with Potatoes
and Apricots
MAKE AHEAD/STORE – Refrigerate
cooled stew, within 2 hours of cooking,
in an airtight container for up to 3 days.
Reheat in a large Dutch oven over a
low heat, adding a splash of water if
necessary, until piping hot all the way
through.
FREEZE – Can be frozen in airtight
containers for up to 3 months. Thaw
overnight in the fridge and reheat
as above.

172. Spicy Mint Lamb Chops with
a Preserved Lemon and Mint Sauce
MAKE AHEAD/STORE – Refrigerate
leftover lamb and sauce, within 2 hours
of cooking, in separate airtight containers
for up to 3 days.

174. Lamb Shanks with Dates
and Pomegranate Molasses
MAKE AHEAD/STORE – To make
ahead, shred meat and refrigerate with the
stew, within 2 hours of making, in airtight
containers. Reheat as directed in recipe
introduction on p.174. Leftovers should be
treated in the same way, but note that the
lamb should be reheated only once.
FREEZE – Shredded lamb and stew
can be frozen in airtight containers for
up to 3 months. Thaw overnight in the
fridge and reheat as above.

177. Bulgur Wheat with Sliced
Almonds and Nigella Seeds
MAKE AHEAD/STORE – It is
not advisable to make ahead but you
can refrigerate leftovers in an airtight
container for up to 3 days. Eat cold.

178. Slow Roast Pork Shoulder with
Caramelized Garlic and Ginger
MAKE AHEAD/STORE – It is not
advisable to make ahead but you can
refrigerate leftovers, within 2 hours of
cooking, in an airtight container for up
to 3 days.

182. Apple Pork Chops with
Sauerkraut Slaw
MAKE AHEAD/STORE – Leftover
slaw can be refrigerated in an airtight
container for 1–2 days.

185. Pork with Prunes, Olives, and Capers
MAKE AHEAD/STORE – Refrigerate cooled stew, within 2 hours of cooking, in an airtight container for up to 3 days. Reheat in a large Dutch oven over a low heat until piping hot all the way through. Reheat only once.
FREEZE – In airtight containers for up to 3 months. Thaw overnight in the fridge and reheat as above.

190. Flat Iron Steak with a Parsley, Shallot, and Caper Salad
MAKE AHEAD/STORE – Steak can be marinated up to 1 day ahead. Refrigerate leftover steak, within 2 hours of cooking, in an airtight container for up to 3 days.

194. Roast Top Round with Caramelized Onions
MAKE AHEAD/STORE – Onions can be cooked up to 5 days ahead. Refrigerate in an airtight container and use as directed. You can refrigerate leftover beef, within 2 hours of cooking, tightly wrapped in foil for up to 2 days. Eat cold.
FREEZE – Leftovers can be frozen, wrapped in an additional layer of foil, for up to 3 months. Thaw overnight in the fridge and check it is thoroughly thawed before serving.

200. Queen of Puddings
MAKE AHEAD/STORE – It is not advisable to make ahead but you can refrigerate leftovers, within 2 hours of cooking, loosely covered with plastic wrap, for up to 2 days (some syrup may form underneath the meringue, but it is fine to eat).
FREEZE – Brioche crumbs can be frozen for up to 3 months ahead, see p.200. Thaw at room temperature for 30 minutes.

204. Apple Gingerjack
MAKE AHEAD/STORE – It is not advisable to make ahead but you can refrigerate leftovers as soon as possible, covered with plastic wrap, for up to 5 days.

206. White Chocolate Cheesecake
MAKE AHEAD/STORE – Refrigerate, covered with plastic wrap, for up to 3 days.
FREEZE – Can be frozen for up to 3 months. Wrap the cheesecake, still in its pan, tightly in a double layer of plastic wrap and a layer of foil. To thaw, unwrap the cheesecake, cover the top loosely with fresh plastic wrap, and leave in the fridge overnight.

208. Rose and Pepper Pavlova with Strawberries and Passionfruit
MAKE AHEAD/STORE – The meringue base can be made 1 day ahead. Store in an airtight container in a cool, dry place (meringue will not keep well in humid or wet weather). Refrigerate leftovers, loosely covered with plastic wrap, for up to 1 day. The meringue will soften as it stands.

210. Chocolate Olive Oil Mousse
MAKE AHEAD/STORE – Mousse can be kept in the fridge, loosely covered with plastic wrap, for up to 3 days. If you need to make ahead, remove from the fridge 40 minutes before serving so that the mousse comes to room temperature. Bear in mind though that the texture won't be quite as consistently light.

214. Warm Blondie Pudding Cake
MAKE AHEAD/STORE – The batter can be mixed up to 1 hour before baking and left in a cool (but not cold) place. Refrigerate leftovers, tightly covered with plastic wrap, for up to 1 week. Eat cold, cut into slabs or squares.

216. Sticky Toffee Pudding
MAKE AHEAD/STORE – Refrigerate leftovers as soon as possible, covered tightly with plastic wrap, for up to 5 days. Store the sponge and extra sauce separately. Reheat sauce gently in a saucepan. The sponge can be reheated on low power in a microwave for 1–2 minutes following the manufacturer's instructions.

219. Maple Roasted Plums with Cinnamon Brown Sugar Yogurt
MAKE AHEAD/STORE – Refrigerate leftovers, storing yogurt and plums separately, in airtight containers, for up to 3 days.

222. Butterscotch Pots
MAKE AHEAD/STORE – The pots will keep in the fridge for up to 3 days. Remove from the fridge about 30 minutes before serving.

224. Passionfruit Ice-Cream Cake with Coconut-Caramel Sauce
MAKE AHEAD/STORE – The sauce can be kept in an airtight container for up to 5 days after having been refrigerated as quickly as possible. Remove from the fridge about an hour before serving, to let it come back to room temperature.
FREEZE – Cake can be frozen for up to 1 month but is at its best within 1 week of making. Sauce can be frozen for up to 3 months. Thaw sauce overnight in fridge and use as above.

229. No-Churn Chocolate Truffle Ice Cream
FREEZE – Best within 1 week of making, but can be kept for up to 1 month in the freezer.

230. No-Churn Bourbon Salted Caramel Ice Cream
FREEZE – Best within 1 week of making, but can be kept for up to 1 month in the freezer.

233. Emergency Brownies
MAKE AHEAD/STORE – It is not advisable to make ahead but you can store leftovers in an airtight container in a cool place for up to 5 days.

234. Pear, Pistachio, and Rose Cake
MAKE AHEAD/STORE – Bake cake 1 day ahead and store in an airtight container in a cool place. Keep leftovers in an airtight container in a cool place for up to 5 days. In hot weather, store in the fridge. The chopped pistachios will soften as the cake stands.

237. Cumin Seed Cake
MAKE AHEAD/STORE – Wrap cooled cake tightly in plastic wrap and store in an airtight container for up to 1 week.
FREEZE – Cake can also be frozen, tightly wrapped in a double layer of plastic wrap and a layer of foil, for up to 3 months. To thaw, unwrap cake, transfer to an airtight container, and leave overnight at room temperature.

238. Lemon Tendercake with Blueberry Compote
MAKE AHEAD/STORE – Compote can be made ahead if refrigerated as quickly as possible, in an airtight container, for up to 2 days. Stir before using. Cake is best eaten on the day it is made. Leftovers can be refrigerated, loosely covered with plastic wrap, for 1 day.
FREEZE – Compote can be frozen for up to 3 months. Thaw overnight in the fridge. Use as above.

242. Victoria Sponge with Cardamom, Marmalade, and Crème Fraîche
MAKE AHEAD/STORE – Cake is best eaten on the day it is made. Refrigerate leftovers of the filled cake, loosely covered with plastic wrap, for up to 3 days. Remove from the fridge about 30 minutes before serving to take the chill off the cake.
FREEZE – Wrap cake layers tightly in a double layer of plastic wrap and a layer of foil and freeze for up to 3 months. To thaw, unwrap and put on a wire rack at room temperature for 2–3 hours. Fill with marmalade and crème fraîche and serve immediately.

244. Chocolate Cake with Coffee Buttercream
MAKE AHEAD/STORE – Bake cake layers 1 day ahead. Cool, carefully wrap in plastic wrap, and store in an airtight container. Fill and frost before serving. The buttercream can be made up to 1 week ahead and stored in an airtight container in the fridge. Remove from the fridge and leave at room temperature until soft enough to spread. Keep leftovers of iced cake in an airtight container in a cool place for up to 5 days.
FREEZE – Carefully wrap un-frosted cake layers in a double layer of plastic wrap and a layer of foil, and freeze for up to 3 months. To thaw, unwrap and put on a wire rack at room temperature for 2–3 hours. Fill and frost with buttercream before serving. The buttercream can also be frozen for up to 3 months. Thaw for several hours at room temperature, until soft enough to spread.

248. Vanilla Layer Cake with Ermine Icing
MAKE AHEAD/STORE – The buttercream can be made up to 4 days ahead. Store in an airtight container in the fridge. To use, let the buttercream come to room temperature, then beat for 3–5 minutes until smooth. Cake layers can be baked 1 day ahead. Cool, wrap in plastic wrap, then store in an airtight container. Refrigerate leftovers for up to 3 days. Remove from the fridge about 30 minutes before serving to take the chill off the cake.
FREEZE – Wrap un-frosted cake layers in a double layer of plastic wrap and a layer of foil and freeze for up to 3 months. To thaw, unwrap cake layers and put on a wire rack for 2–3 hours. Frost before serving. The buttercream can also be frozen in an airtight container for up to 3 months. Thaw overnight in the fridge and use as above.

252. Ginger and Walnut Carrot Cake
MAKE AHEAD/STORE – The cake can be baked up to 2 days ahead. Wrap in a layer of plastic wrap and keep in an airtight container, frost before serving. Frosting can be made a day ahead and stored in an airtight container in the fridge. Remove from fridge and leave at room temperature until soft enough to spread. Store leftovers in an airtight container in a cool place for up to 5 days.
FREEZE – Wrap un-iced cake in a double layer of plastic wrap and a layer of foil, and freeze for up to 3 months. To thaw, unwrap and put on a wire rack at room temperature for 4–5 hours. Top with frosting before serving.

254. Raspberry-Flecked Sour Cream Cake
MAKE AHEAD/STORE – Bake cake 1 day ahead. Cool, wrap in plastic wrap, and store in an airtight container. Ice and decorate before serving. Store leftovers in an airtight container for up to 5 days.
FREEZE – Wrap un-iced cake in a double layer of plastic wrap and a layer of foil, and freeze for up to 3 months. To thaw,

unwrap the cake and stand it on a wire rack at room temperature for about 2 hours. Ice and decorate cake before serving.

256. Scented Citrus Cake
MAKE AHEAD/STORE – Bake cake 1 day ahead. Cool and store in the springform pan, tightly wrapped in plastic wrap or in an airtight container, in a cool place overnight. Ice before serving. Store leftovers in an airtight container in a cool place for up to 5 days.
FREEZE – Wrap un-iced cake in a double layer of plastic wrap and a layer of foil, and freeze for up to 3 months. Freeze the cake on the springform base for extra protection. To thaw, unwrap and leave on a wire rack at room temperature for 3–4 hours. Ice before serving.

258. Sunken Chocolate Amaretto Cake with Crumbled Amaretti Cream
MAKE AHEAD/STORE – Bake cake 1 day ahead. Store in an airtight container in a cool place. Dust with cocoa before serving. Store leftover cake in an airtight container in a cool place for up to 2 days.
FREEZE – Wrap cake in a double layer of plastic wrap and a layer of foil, and freeze for up to 3 months. Freeze the cake on the springform base for extra protection. To thaw, unwrap and leave on a wire rack at room temperature for 3–4 hours. Dust with cocoa before serving.

260. Coconut Snowball Cake
MAKE AHEAD/STORE – Bake cake layers 1 day ahead. Cool, wrap in plastic wrap, and store in an airtight container. Fill and frost before serving. The cake should be eaten within 2 hours of frosting and leftovers refrigerated and eaten within 24 hours. The frosting will lose some of its airiness as it stands. If possible leave the cake uncovered in the fridge, making sure it does not touch any other foods.

FREEZE – Freeze un-frosted cake layers, carefully wrapped in a double layer of plastic wrap and a layer of foil, for up to 3 months. To thaw, unwrap and put on a wire rack at room temperature for 2–3 hours. Fill and frost before serving.

265. Double Chocolate and Pumpkin Seed Cookies
MAKE AHEAD/STORE – The cookie dough can be made up to 3 days ahead and stored, covered, in the fridge. Let the dough come to room temperature (about 30 minutes) before forming and baking the cookies. To store, keep in an airtight container for up to 5 days.
FREEZE – Unbaked dough can be formed into mounds and frozen on a baking sheet lined with parchment paper. Once solid, transfer to a resealable plastic bag and freeze for up to 3 months. Bake directly from frozen, adding 1–2 minutes to the baking time.

266. Forgotten Cookies
MAKE AHEAD/STORE – Best eaten within 24 hours but can keep up to 5 days. Store in airtight containers, but don't put too many in each container as they crush easily. The cookies will soften as they are stored, more quickly in humid conditions.
FREEZE – Can also be frozen in rigid airtight containers, with layers of parchment paper in between the cookies, for up to 1 month. To thaw, transfer cookies to a plate and leave at room temperature for 30–60 minutes, then eat as soon as possible, as they soften fairly quickly once thawed.

268. Turmeric and Ginger Vodka
MAKE AHEAD/STORE – After straining, store in a cool, dry place, out of bright light, for up to 1 year.

273. Grapefruit Margarita
MAKE AHEAD/STORE – For a pitcherful stir the tequila, orange liqueur, and grapefruit juice together in the pitcher. Cover and refrigerate for up to 24 hours. Stir again before serving and pour into glasses filled with ice cubes.

NOTES
The following recipes contain raw or lightly cooked eggs, and are not suitable for people with compromised or weak immune systems, such as younger children, the elderly, or pregnant women:

14. **Turkish Eggs**
20. **Black Pudding Hash** with Fried Egg
22. **Golden Egg Curry**
115. **Golden Garlic Mayonnaise**
210. **Chocolate Olive Oil Mousse**
260. **Coconut Snowball Cake**

Flour measurements are spooned and leveled, and brown sugar measurements are firmly packed. Vegetable, legume, and grain cup measurements are approximated.

INDEX

–285–

ACKNOWLEDGMENTS

I feel immensely lucky to be able to say that there are many people I want to thank here, and top of my list are Hettie Potter and Zoe Wales, whose hard work and support make them the book's – and my – truest allies. My gratitude is fathomless. No book of mine could come into being without Caz Hildebrand, either. And Jonathan Lovekin's beautiful photography also ushered *At My Table* into life. But I also want to sing out glad thanks to Clara Farmer, Gail Rebuck, and Rowan Yapp at Chatto & Windus, Harry Bingham and Julie Martin at Here Design, Fiona Golfar, Mark Hutchinson, Zuzana Kratka, Sanjana Lovekin, Yasmin Othman, and Caroline Stearns, as well as to Apacuka Ceramics, Le Creuset, La Fromagerie, KitchenAid, Netherton Foundry, Nordic Ware, SkandiHus, and Summerill & Bishop. And, as ever, a particular thank you, too, to my fishmonger, Rex Goldsmith of The Chelsea Fishmonger, my butchers, Adam and Daniel of H. G. Walters, and my greengrocer, Andreas of Andreas Veg.

But my deepest gratitude is to my beloved friend and literary agent, Ed Victor. This book's dedication originally read "To Ed Victor, without whom…" Now I have to change it, heartbreakingly, so that it is dedicated to his memory.